FAITH AND FILM

FAITH AND FILM

Theological Themes at the Cinema

Bryan P. Stone

CHALICE PRESS

ST. LOUIS, MISSOURI

Cover design and illustration: Michael Foley
Art direction: Michael H. Domínguez
Interior design: Wynn Younker

Visit Chalice Press on the World Wide Web at
www.chalicepress.com

10 9 8 7 6 5 4   06 07 08 09 10

Library of Congress Cataloging–in–Publication Data

Stone, Bryan P., 1959–
    Faith and Film : theological themes at the cinema / by Bryan P. Stone.
        p.   cm.
    Includes bibliographical references and index.
    ISBN 13: 978-0-827210-27-1
    ISBN 10: 0-827210-27-2
    1. Motion pictures—Religious aspects—Christianity.   2. Jesus Christ—In motion pictures.   I. Title.
    PN1995.5 .S76   1999   99–050537
    791.43'682—dc21   C1P

Printed in the United States of America

For Cheryl

Contents

Acknowledgments

There are a number of people to be thanked in a project of this nature. The idea for such a book began during my teaching appointment at Azusa Pacific University in Azusa, California. There I was given a generous Creative Education Project grant to conduct research and begin to develop a course that would employ film as a means of teaching theology. I am grateful to the Azusa Pacific University community and to the students who served as thoughtful critics in the project and who gave valuable feedback and assistance. I am also thankful to the faculty, staff, and students at Boston University School of Theology, where I now teach, who have continued to dialogue with me about the relationship between faith and film and who have therefore also shaped this book.

To my wife, Cheryl, who has watched more movies with me than she probably cares to admit or remember and whose ideas and good advice for this book I have tried to follow, I lovingly dedicate this book.

The Apostles' Creed

I believe in God, the Father almighty,
creator of heaven and earth.

I believe in Jesus Christ, his only Son, our Lord.
He was conceived by the Holy Spirit and
born of the Virgin Mary.
He suffered under Pontius Pilate,
was crucified, died, and was buried.
He descended to the dead.
On the third day he rose again.
He ascended into heaven,
and is seated at the right hand of the Father.
He will come again to judge the living and the dead.

I believe in the Holy Spirit,
the holy catholic church,
the communion of saints,
the forgiveness of sins,
the resurrection of the body
and the life everlasting.

Introduction

Cinema, Theology, and the "Signs of the Times"

In Matthew's gospel, Jesus chides the religious leaders of his day for their inability to discern the "signs of the times" (16:3). They had been trained in reading and understanding scripture, but they could not interpret the world around them. They failed to understand that history is itself a kind of text and that it is as important to understand the human predicament as it is to understand the word of God that is addressed to that predicament. In fact, it is doubtful whether we can ever adequately read and understand scripture, given an inability to read and understand the world.

A fundamental assumption of this book is that what is especially needed within the Christian movement today is vigorous and sustained thinking about both the gospel *and* the world, about scripture *and* human existence, about text *and* context. When we read the Bible but are not able to read the world, we risk reducing the gospel to either a *weapon* or a *toy*. In the first case, the gospel is hurled at the world like a spear, brandished like a sword, or wielded like a club. It is a clumsy and uninvited word—one that does not speak to us but merely stands over us and against us. It may sting, but it doesn't heal. In the second case, the gospel is a plaything—an amusing distraction to be played with, fondled, and polished. It has no relevance or function in a world of corporate mergers, unemployment, and global commerce. It is little more than a topic on the Internet or a slogan on a bumper sticker. It answers questions few people are asking.

We Christians sometimes forget that the gospel is virtually mean-ingless apart from the human projects, loyalties, and concerns that are the medium through which it is rendered both intelligible and interesting. One of our most important tasks today is to learn better to read the world along with the gospel—to hear more clearly the questions the world is asking and to provoke the world to ask new questions. This is the essence of Christian theology, not merely the study of scripture text but of worldly context. Theology always de-mands an intimate familiarity with both.

Given this double requirement of theology, it should not be too difficult to make the case that the cinema can be an important dialogue partner for Christians who are interested in thinking seri-ously about their faith. In a sense, the cinema is a source of revela-tion—not necessarily about the nature of God, the significance of Christ, or the path to salvation (though it certainly does illuminate those topics from time to time). Rather, the cinema is regularly and quite amazingly a source of revelation about ourselves and our world—about the "signs of the times." The cinema reveals what we value as human beings, our hopes and our fears. It asks our deepest questions, expresses our mightiest rage, and reflects our most basic dreams.

Linking Christian faith and theology with the arts is not some-thing entirely new, of course. Christians have enjoyed a rich history of leaning heavily on the arts in order to carry out the tasks of bearing witness to the Christian faith. Just think of the impressive cathedrals of the Middle Ages that attempted to express Christian truth through their stained glass, handsome murals, ornate ceilings, and soaring arches. Architecture, acoustics, the careful use of light and shadows, even the smell of incense—all these have served as media for the communication of the gospel.

But the role of the aesthetic has become diminished in the face of a rationalistic religion that reduced faith to dogma and truth to propositions. It would be no exaggeration to say that in recent cen-turies the printed word in theology has predominated over imagi-nation, drama, myth, pictures, and storytelling. And yet few, if any, of our most fundamental Christian convictions can be reduced to words on a printed page. There remains in human beings a deep hunger for images, sound, pictures, music, and myth. Film offers us a creative language—an imaginative language of movement and sound—that can bridge the gap between the rational and the aesthetic, the sacred and the secular, the church and the world, and thereby throw open fresh new windows on a very old gospel.

The Cinema: Mirror, Window, or Lens?

I grew up in a conservative Christian denomination that taught that it was wrong to go to the movies. The cinema was spelled *s-i-n-ema,* and Hollywood, we were taught, was an industry that was as opposed to Christian values as anything could be. Nothing short of absolute nonattendance at the cinema was understood to be the appropriate response of Christians to Hollywood and its values. My church's position was not intended to be a political statement, nor was it a strategy to bring about change in the industry such as a boycott would be. It was simply an expression of a fundamental desire on the part of its members to keep themselves unstained by the world. They had the idea that time spent in the cinema was not just harmless entertainment, but that through the power of images what is actually happening is that the mind is being shaped and transformed by the values, ideas, and desires of the filmmakers. My church had the notion that subconsciously and cumulatively, through repeated attendance at the cinema, what you saw was literally what you "got."

In junior high, my parents allowed me to slip by the rules and go on school field trips to see such movies as *Romeo and Juliet* and *Julius Caesar.* Somehow sex, violence, revenge, and bigotry are easier to take when packaged in Elizabethan English. Films like these, however, began for me a love of the cinema that has grown stronger and stronger through the years. I still know a few members in my denomination who, even today, refuse to visit the cinema, but Hollywood has found alternate ways into their lives and homes through video stores and cable movie channels. It is the rare individual these days who is able to pull off total abstinence, not only of the cinema but also of HBO, Cinemax, and Blockbuster Video.

However difficult in practice it might be to maintain a consistent and thoroughgoing witness against the motion picture industry, we should be cautious about too easily dismissing such conservative Christian attitudes as simply quirky or fanatic. It may be that they, more than other Christian groups, were able to perceive accurately the awesome ability of film to shape our lives and culture. At least one of the things these Christians were saying was that it is naive to believe that film, either as an art form or a medium for communication, is somehow unbiased. The cinema may function both as a *mirror* and as a *window*, but it is primarily a *lens*. We see only what the camera lets us see, and we hear only what the writer has scripted. Movies do not merely portray a world; they propagate a worldview. A good illustration of this insight can be found in the 1976 film *Network,* when newscaster Howard Beale, the angry prophet of the airwaves, makes the following indictment against television (an indictment that could easily be extended to the cinema):

> Right now, there is a whole, an entire generation that never knew anything that didn't come out of this tube! This tube is the gospel, the ultimate revelation; this tube can make or break presidents, popes, prime ministers… You're beginning to believe the illusions we're spinning here, you're beginning to believe that the tube is reality and your own lives are unreal! You do! Why, whatever the tube tells you: you dress like the tube, you eat like the tube, you raise your children like the tube, you even think like the tube! This is mass madness, you maniacs! In God's name, you people are the real thing, WE are the illusion!

The cinema is a double-edged sword. It helps us see what we might not otherwise have seen, but it also shapes what and how we see. Perhaps my denomination was right! There is truth in its intuition that the industry as a whole and cumulatively *can* be antithetical to Christian values. But that does not mean—and here my agreement with the tradition ends—that wholesale abstinence is or ever has been the proper response of Christians to the cinema. The worldview and values propagated by the cinema—however subtly or implicitly this may occur—must be critiqued through a posture of constructive engagement rather than a silent standoff. And this critique must be rigorous and extended far beyond the narrow scope of values and behaviors typically critiqued by standard rating systems concerned only with whether a film features profanity, nudity, or violence. Today's Christian must also ask about the way in which Hollywood film conventions teach us to understand and relate to difference in our society—the outsider, the foreigner, the gay, or the minority. And what about the way white culture continues to be made the norm in films? Or the way patterns of consumption and materialism are treated as normative? Or the way religious faith is trivialized and marginalized—the way it is reduced to a caricature? Or the way the role of women is perpetuated as one of scenery and as foil for the adventures of men? For all Hollywood's purported liberalism and loose morality, its standard film conventions are actually quite conservative. Hollywood does not tell us overtly that it is all right to be racist, sexist, or xenophobic, but by being repeatedly portrayed on screen such attitudes, behaviors, and values are reinforced as "natural" and "right."[1]

There is no single person, entity, organization, institution, or power in our society today that even comes close to rivaling the power of film and television to shape our faith, values, and behavior. Learning to live and think as Christians in our time requires learning to engage media and culture as Christians. Together we must become aware of the power of images and find both the tools to explore and critique these images as well as the opportunities to shape that which so thoroughly shapes us. This means, among other things, that the relationship between film and theology cannot be solely a relationship in which theology merely uses film to illustrate or advance its own ideas. We must also become more responsible as Christians for engaging film theologically—for attending to its tacit faith claims and critiquing its implicit pretense of mirroring reality. The relationship between Christian theology and popular film is, in short, an interfaith dialogue.

What follows in this book is an attempt at just this kind of dialogue. True dialogue, of course, runs in two directions. In one direction, there are points where we will find that film is able to help us think more imaginatively about the meaning of Christian faith—to grasp its decisiveness for our own situation in fresh, new, and creative ways. In a worship service I attended recently, the congregation was being lulled to sleep in typical fashion by the pastor as he trudged along through his sermon. At some point in the sermon, however, he tried to illustrate his point by alluding to a recent film that had just started playing at the neighborhood theater. Never mind that the pastor's name was neither Siskel nor Ebert. The entire congregation was suddenly interested in what the preacher was saying, and each person began to sit up in the pew, almost in unison. It was as if the man had begun using a magic vocabulary that enchanted, invited, and intrigued everyone within range of hearing. People love the movies! It is one of the central theses of this book that this love can be translated into a new opportunity for teaching, illustrating, and enriching Christian faith claims.

At other points in the following pages, however, the dialogue between theology and cinema must travel in the opposite direction. If popular film can shed new light on traditional Christian faith claims, the Christian faith also wants to shed some light on both the explicit messages and implicit assumptions of popular film. The underlying faith claims of film must be challenged. In some cases, they must be exposed as inadequate, false, and even dehumanizing. Even here, however, the cinema can serve to make our faith stronger as we distinguish the Christian faith from other inviting options.

The Apostles' Creed

Creeds are concise statements of what people believe. At their worst, they are constrictive, narrow hedges that box believers in and can even serve as a source of division, intolerance, and oppression in the Christian community. At their best, however, creeds can be useful devices for teaching and worship, and a way of connecting us with our past and with the best thinking of those who have gone before us. The most important creeds in Christian history were the product of prayer, contemplation, debate, controversy, and even intense political pressure. They did not drop from the sky ready-made any more than did the Bible. They developed over years of thinking theologically as a community of faith. What is known today as the Apostles' Creed is a distillation of much of what was taught by the earliest witnesses to Jesus. In fact, there is an ancient legend that each of the twelve apostles contributed a phrase to the creed.[2] More than likely, however, the actual words of the creed date back only to the early part of the third century, when they appeared in the form of a three-part question in the context of baptism. Some two hundred years after Christ, a Roman writer named Hippolytus detailed the profession of faith made by candidates for baptism, and it is here that we find the beginnings of what would come to be known as the Apostles' Creed:

> Do you believe in God the Father almighty?
> And he who is to be baptised shall say:
> I believe.
> Let him forthwith baptise him at once, having his hand laid
>   upon his head. And after this let him say:
> Do you believe in Christ Jesus, the Son of God,
> Who was born of the Holy Spirit and the Virgin Mary,
> Who was crucified in the days of Pontius Pilate,
> And died,
> And rose the third day living from the dead,
> And ascended into the heavens,
> And sat down at the right hand of the Father,
> And will come to judge the living and the dead?
> And when he says: I believe, let him baptise him the second
>   time and again let him say:
> Do you believe in the Holy Spirit, in the Holy Church, and
>   the resurrection of the flesh?
> And he who is being baptised shall say: I believe. And so let
>   him baptise him the third time.[3]

Although the creed did not appear in its present Latin form until about the eighth century, a close relative known as the "Old Roman Creed" appeared in Greek in 340 C.E. Early on in the church, during Lent, the bishop would explain the creed phrase by phrase to new converts and to young people who were going through catechism and preparing to be baptized. They, in turn, would be expected to memorize the creed and repeat it back to the bishop. Thus, the creed served as a tool for instruction in the faith and as a common story or narrative that served as a point of Christian identification and unity.

Although the creed is not scripture, it has served for at least sixteen centuries as a short yet comprehensive summary of Christian beliefs. Many churches include the Apostles' Creed as a central part of their liturgy and worship or as a vehicle for evangelism and instruction, an instrument to help the faithful to remain anchored. In more than one instance it has even been set to music. That is not to say that all Christians at all times have allowed their doctrine to be defined in terms of the creed or have used it as an instrument for distinguishing between orthodoxy and heresy. Traditions that are historically anticreedal, for example, have been especially wary of giving to this or any other creed any kind of dogmatic authority.

Certainly it is also the case that not all Christians have agreed with every phrase of the creed or interpreted each phrase in the same way. For example, the phrase "He descended to the dead" is troubling to some Christians who can find no clear scriptural support for such a journey, while others find in the phrase an important reference to the fact that Jesus came to save all people, including those who had already died. Some see in the phrase an affirmation that Jesus really did die a full human death and thus, in terms of the worldview of the day, did indeed sink fully to the realm of the dead.

Wherever we land on the matter of creeds, however, perhaps the Apostles' Creed can still serve an important role for the church by assisting us to reflect on what we mean when we call ourselves "Christians" today. Perhaps the creed, regardless of whatever short-comings it may have, has enough universality and longevity to teach us something about Christian faith and about the kinds of beliefs and loyalties implied in that faith. At least, that is the conviction and the prayer of this book.

The organization of the book is such that each phrase from the creed will be examined in the order in which it appears. This should not lead us to believe, however, that the several phrases of the creed are to be viewed as a menu of individual beliefs from which we might pick and choose. In fact, it is difficult to know how to break down the creed into distinct and separate articles of faith.[4] It may be that the unity of the creed is viewed better as the single plot of a story rather than as a catalog of Christian beliefs. As Nicholas Lash says,

> There may be many things which, as Christians, we believe, but we seriously misunderstand the grammar of the creed if we suppose its primary purpose to be that of furnishing a list of them. To say the creed is to say, not many things, but one. To say the creed is to perform an act which has one object: right worship of the mystery of God. To say the creed is to confess, beyond all conflict and confusion, our trust in

One who makes and heals the world and who makes all things one.[5]

The creed, then, is a way of affirming one thing, not a list of things. The creed is the expression of a singular faith in and allegiance to the God of Jesus experienced today through the power of the Holy Spirit. The purpose of the creed does have a personal dimension and may even be considered to be autobiographical in nature. The creed is an affirmation of what *I* as a Christian believe. But the creed is also communal. We are sharing a larger story when we confess the creed. Indeed, the creed is an invitation to share a particular kind of life together. It provides Christians with a common language that binds us together and stakes out a common path that we agree to walk along. In a world where there is such confusion about what Christians believe, even among Christians themselves, perhaps the rediscovery of the creed can serve as a resource both for furthering Christian understanding and unity and for communicating Christian truth to a world that waits to hear it.

How to Use the Book

This book has been written for those who are interested in thinking critically about the Christian faith, whether as individuals or in small gatherings such as classes, congregations, study groups, or fellowships. I suggest that the best way to use the book is first to view the film before reading each chapter—preferably with others who can engage in dialogue about it afterward. At the end of each chapter I have provided questions for reflection that attempt to stimulate this dialogue and to initiate theological reflection on the films as a transition to the chapters themselves. Therefore, the discussion questions will be used most profitably after seeing the film, but prior to reading the chapter. The questions all typically receive some treatment within the chapter itself, so that reading the chapter first may tend to dampen or control a discussion that might otherwise occur. Furthermore, the chapters also include significant "spoiler" information that can be irritating to those who have not yet seen the film.

There is no science in knowing which films to interface with the various sections of the creed. Though most chapters focus on only one film, in many instances there are a number of films that could have been fruitful dialogue partners. In chapters 5 and 8 I treat a trio of films together, and if you are using the book in a small group, I leave to you the choice of which film to view. I might suggest, however, *The Gospel According to St. Matthew* for chapter 5 because it is such an unusual and critically acclaimed approach to the story of Jesus, and *Powder* for chapter 8 because of its moving portrayal of a secular ascension.

At the end of each chapter, I have provided a list of related films that may also be of interest, and at the end of the book is a list of film summaries, including Motion Picture Association of America (MPAA) rating, running time, and other information. Clearly some of the films are not suitable for all audiences, though it is virtually impossible to tie a film's MPAA rating to its value for theological dialogue. I have tried to use films that represent a variety of genres (comedy, horror, science fiction, biography, drama, etc.). A few non–English language films have been chosen as well. I have tried to use films that are more or less popular—almost all the films included did well at the box office. Whether we like it or not, popular films have the ability to register the hopes and dreams, fears and anxieties of a broad cross section of our culture. Why such films appeal to so many people is, in fact, a consideration worthy of investigation in its own right. Most of the films are relatively easy to find in a neighborhood video store, with the exception of *The Gospel According to St. Matthew*, which may be a bit more difficult to locate. Some libraries, especially college and university libraries, are good places to search for it, and I was even able to purchase a copy easily and cheaply through an Internet book dealer.

NOTES

[1]Margaret R. Miles, *Seeing and Believing* (Boston: Beacon Press, 1997), 27.

[2]J. N. D. Kelly, *Early Christian Creeds*, 3d Ed. (Essex, U.K.: Longman, 1972), 3.

[3]Gregory Dix, editor, *The Apostolic Tradition of St. Hippolytus of Rome* (New York: Macmillan, 1937), 36–37.

[4]There is a long history of Christian thinkers who have attempted to divide the Apostles' Creed into various principal parts. Aquinas distinguished two sets of seven clauses, while Erasmus criticized such a division as departing from the traditional twelvefold schema with its roots in the legend of the Creed's apostolic origins. Luther, like many modern interpreters, emphasized the trinitarian structure

of the creed so that there are really only three primary articles of faith—one pertaining to the Father (God the Creator), one pertaining to the Son (God the Redeemer), and one pertaining to the Holy Spirit (God the Sanctifier); cf. Bernard Marthaler, *The Creed,* 2d ed. (Mystic, Conn.: Twenty-Third Publications, 1993), 11–13.

⁵Nicholas Lash, *Believing Three Ways in One God: A Reading of the Apostles' Creed* (Notre Dame, Ind.: University of Notre Dame Press, 1992), 16.

"I believe"

 *Contact* [1]

In keeping with the trinitarian structure of the Apostles' Creed, the simple phrase "I believe" stands at the beginning of each of its three major sections:"I believe in the Father,""I believe in the Son," "I believe in the Holy Spirit."The two words remind us that to be a Christian is to hold a common set of beliefs—fundamental convictions shared by believers throughout the past twenty centuries. For the Christian, however, *believing* is far from just a mental activity. It is about loyalties, allegiances, and values.To believe is to hold deep convictions about the meaning and purpose of our lives and the very nature of ultimate reality, but it is also an active way of living together in the world.To believe is to *exercise* faith.

We begin our survey of the creed by examining a science fiction film that focuses centrally on matters of faith and belief, *Contact* (1997), directed by Robert Zemeckis (of *Forrest Gump* fame). As a modern genre, science fiction—whether in literature, film, or television—is uniquely suited for dealing with questions of faith.At first glance, we might take science fiction to be a distraction, a flight of fancy and escape from the real world.When science fiction first began to appear almost a hundred years ago, it was considered little more than the product of end-of-the-century anxiety. Since that time, however, it has served as an important avenue for dealing with heavy questions such as the shape of ultimate reality, the meaning of life, and the place of human beings in the cosmos. Though religion and religious faith are not always an explicit preoccupation of contemporary film, it is not unusual to find science fiction dealing head-on with issues that have religious importance as an underlying and recurring theme. *Contact* boldly places the question of religious faith and its relationship to science at its front and center.

Contact ranked eleventh in the top grossing films of 1997, securing for itself a respectable position in contemporary American culture so far as popular film goes. The film is based on the late Carl Sagan's novel by the same name that imagines the personal, religious, and political impact of an extraterrestrial encounter—a question that is certainly worth entertaining, especially with regard to its theological implications. Anyone who has paid attention to the work of Carl Sagan will easily recognize his perennial interests throughout the film. Sagan, an outspoken atheist who wrote more than two dozen books, hundreds of articles, and hosted the 1980 PBS series *Cosmos,* was enormously successful in his lifetime at popularizing science and giving the search for extraterrestrial intelligence a measure of scientific respectability. Though Sagan had no place in his worldview for traditional religion and popular notions of God, he had a deep appreciation for the unresolvable mysteries of the universe. Sagan was actively involved in the transition of *Contact* from book to screenplay until his death at age 62 in December 1996. Toward the beginning of the film, the central character of *Contact*, Eleanor "Ellie" Arroway, asks her dad whether he thinks there are people on other planets. In a line that is something of a Sagan mantra, her father replies, "I don't know…but I guess I'd say if it is just us…seems like an awful waste of space."

It is difficult to watch the film without being impressed by its special effects—especially the very beginning of the film where we are graphically transported backward away from the planet Earth for an incredible ride through the universe. However, *Contact* is much more subtle and intelligent on the "alien" side of things than other recent films, and it does have a way of drawing the viewer in where the dimension of science is concerned. Roger Ebert refers to *Contact* as "the smartest and most absorbing story about extraterrestrial intelligence since *Close Encounters of the Third Kind*."[2] Of course, that may not be saying much, since few science fiction films over the last two decades have taken it upon themselves to rise above standard plots that include lots of people getting "slimed" by aliens, and cosmic cowboys chasing interplanetary bad guys throughout the galaxy.

It is refreshing to see a popular film deal with issues such as the existence of God, the meaning of faith, and the relationship between science and religion, rather than how to kill off strange-looking creatures. Unfortunately, this preoccupation with heavy questions can cause the film to become preachy and to attempt to be overly profound. At one point in the film, where the central character is making a case for research funding, the film has her describe her quest for making contact with aliens as "something that just might end up being the most profoundly impactful moment for humanity…for the history of history." Here is a film that strains under the weight of its own pretensions to be dealing with the "big

Contact: © Warner Bros. Inc., Courtesy MoMA

issues" (and, no, there is no such word as "impactful" in the English language).

In brief, the film is about Ellie Arroway (Jodie Foster), a zealous radio astronomer who discovers a pulsing signal originating from the star system Vega, some twenty-six light years away (later in the film we see an Elvis look-alike holding a sign that says "Viva Las Vega"). The signal contains instructions for building a star-transport, and most of the film traces the political, scientific, and religious complications that develop in response to the alien signal and Ellie's strong desire to be the one to go on the transport. Introduced into the story to provide roadblocks for Ellie are a glory-hogging science advisor to the president (Tom Skerritt) and a paranoid national security advisor (James Woods). Ellie is an atheist because she doesn't find any empirical evidence for the existence of God; but because the film develops her character so well, even the most devout theists will find themselves liking her and taking her side.

Ellie finally gets to take the transport, and after traveling through galactic wormholes at cosmic speeds, she encounters an alien who, strangely enough, appears in the form of her father (I can just see Freud with a broad smile across his face). The alien has few answers for Ellie's questions and can only give her hints of the evolutionary process that has for millions of years brought them to this point. The alien doesn't even know how the transport system got there in the first place. Nonetheless, he comforts Ellie with the following words of wisdom:

> You're an interesting species, an interesting mix. You're capable of such beautiful dreams and such horrible nightmares. You feel so lost, so cut off, so alone. See, in all our searching, the only thing we've found that makes the emptiness bearable...is each other.

Twenty-six light years, and all we humans get for the effort is a cure for interplanetary angst! Still, an understated alien encounter is refreshing, given some of the outlandish portrayals in other science fiction movies. The film quickly turns to what is perhaps its most important segment—not the alien encounter, but Ellie's return to earth. To her fellow earthlings it appears that her star-transport never left—such is the nature of interstellar travel. Ellie is now left having to explain her experience not merely in the face of a lack of evidence, but in the face of controverting evidence. Ellie the atheist is reduced to the status of those poor religious folk who have no proof for their claims, but must simply live by faith and bear witness to their life-changing experiences in an unbelieving world.

The other central character, Palmer Joss (played by Matthew McConaughey), shows up early in the film during Ellie's research at the Arecibo radio telescope site in Puerto Rico. McConaughey is completely unconvincing as a kind of New Age ex-Catholic theologian who got his Master of Divinity degree, dropped out of seminary, and is now working on a book about how technology affects third-world cultures. Later in the film, we discover he has written another book titled *Losing Faith*, an indictment of modern culture, which has lost its sense of direction and meaning despite its advances in science, technology, and creature comforts. According to Palmer, "We shop at home, we surf the Web, at the same time we're emptier."

Palmer is supposed to represent faith in the film, and Ellie, of course, represents science. Their flirtations are the flirtations between science and faith. When they hold hands or kiss, we are watching the potential union of science and faith. And in a scene that is loaded with theological potential, faith gives science his number, but science never calls! The problem, however, is that we don't get to know Palmer well enough to understand, let alone identify with, his version of faith, so that throughout the movie the "faith" that collides with and sometimes colludes with science remains abstract, mushy, and meaningless. We do know that Palmer couldn't, as he says, "live with the whole celibacy thing." He tells Ellie, "You could call me a man of the cloth…without the cloth." Following the standard Hollywood convention for communicating to viewers that the two have established a close, caring relationship, they fall into bed for a one-night stand, never to see each other again until four years later after Ellie has tuned in to the alien signal. By this time, Palmer has become, as Larry King describes him, "author and theologian…spiritual counselor of sorts and a recent fixture at the White House," or, according to *The New York Times*, "God's diplomat."

As a film that deals with the question of the existence of God, both of its central characters, Ellie and Palmer, supply the typical arguments for their respective positions on the topic, and while their arguments are by no means profound, it is extraordinary to see a popular film even allow itself to deal with such questions explicitly. Where the film gets muddled, however, is, first, in its attempt to portray authentic religious faith, and, second, in its attempt to interface science with religious faith (which, of course, is a muddle that is the byproduct of the first muddle). Perhaps the film does not really understand religious faith, or maybe, while pretending to remain neutral on the question, it so implicitly disagrees with religious faith that it finds it difficult to write well for it.

It is tempting to suggest that it is Carl Sagan's well-known atheism that is the culprit here, but the truth of the matter is that authentic religious faith is notoriously difficult to depict accurately on screen. Try to think of how many films you have ever watched that even attempted such a depiction, much less pulled it off successfully. It is much easier to resort to caricature and distortion. Two of the films we will examine later in this book, *The Mission* and *Dead Man Walking,* come to mind as moderately successful in this regard, but such films are rare. Even films that are explicitly religious, such as some of the more well-known Hollywood epics on the life of Jesus, are, as we shall see in chapter 5, notoriously shallow when it comes to portraying religious motivation and faith. Through the vehicle of the Palmer Joss character, *Contact* tries not to yield to the standard Hollywood convention of trivializing religion by presenting persons of faith as misinformed, confused, ineffective, fundamentalist, or fanatical. But it is not at all clear that it succeeds in doing this with Palmer, and, in the case of three other less prominent instances of religious figures in the film, it finally does succumb to traditional Hollywood conventions altogether (and that doesn't even count the man holding the "Jesus is an alien" sign halfway through the movie!).

The first of these figures is a priest who, in the beginning of the film, attempts to console Ellie, age 9, after her father has died. The priest tells her, "Ellie, I know it's hard to understand this now, but we aren't always meant to know the reasons why things happen the

way they do. Sometimes we just have to accept it as God's will."
Ellie responds matter-of-factly, "I should have kept some medicine
in the downstairs bathroom...then I could have gotten to it sooner,"
and the priest is left with a helpless, confused stare on his face. It has
now gotten to the point in popular film that if you see a man with
a clerical collar, you can count on his being morally reprobate, in-
flexibly ruthless, or, in this case, sincere but intellectually helpless.

The second religious figure is Richard Rank, leader of the
Conservative Coalition, who is thrown into the mix now and again
to blabber this and that about not knowing whether the aliens have
any moral values or to criticize science for "intruding into matters
of faith." This is meant, of course, to be a parody of Ralph Reed and
his conservative political action group, the Christian Coalition. The
parody is made all the more biting by the casting of Rob Lowe (not
exactly the epitome of righteousness). Finally, there is the fanatical
cult member with a crucifix draped around his neck who blames
science for all the world's woes and subsequently tries to nuke the
entire project. But for what reason? "What we do, we do for the
goodness of all mankind. This won't be understood—not now—
but the apocalypse to come will vindicate our faith." In other words,
no answer is to be given. Instead the film merely falls back on one
of the standard film conventions for portraying religious faith, a
mixture of fanaticism and irrationality. Not that some future contact with extraterrestrial intelligence wouldn't occasion some very
real conflict and tension between science and religion. One need
not think long about the central doctrines of Christianity such as
the significance of Christ, the meaning of salvation, or the nature
and destiny of human beings to realize that each of them would be
thrown into a tizzy with the advent of aliens; but, of course, these
are not explored in the film. Rather, the focus of the faith versus
science tension is an entirely antitechnology predilection.

So, then, are these the only candidates to be found for what it
means to be a person of "faith": the useless priest, the political
moralizer, the irrational fanatic, or the whatever-Palmer-Joss-is? Apparently so. *Contact* is a good example of how Hollywood creates
and maintains popular attitudes toward religion and religious "faith"
whether it intends to or not. What we find in *Contact* is an explicit

message about science and religion that attempts a neutrality and maybe even a positive cooperation between the two. On the implicit level, however (the level where film conventions operate most powerfully), we find what is true of many popular films—a consensus that traditional religious faith is deeply untrustworthy and to be placed at the margins of culture, if not rejected altogether.

Furthermore, because of the implicit messages the film conveys to its viewers about the nature of religious faith, it never really is able to make the jump it wants to with regard to the relationship between that very faith and science. In the end, faith is not allowed to stand on its own two feet but is instead reduced to a caricature. As a by-product, even the question of God's existence is treated throughout the film as if it were logically parallel to the question of alien existence. It is just this confusion that an authentically Christian faith can never allow. The existence of God is not at all similar in structure to the question of whether there are aliens. The latter will always be an empirical question that is answerable, at least in principle, by empirical methods of discovery, while the question of God's existence is in a different category altogether. Such confusion is almost as laughable as hearing once again of the Soviet cosmonaut who, having attained space orbit, proudly boasted that he saw no God. What we have here is a mixing of categories and a misunderstanding of the nature of faith.

Faith and the Creed

In the Latin used by the early church, faith was translated by the verb *credo* (I believe) and the noun *fides* (faith). Both words still indicated a sense of trust, pledge, allegiance, or commitment. In fact, the word *credo* (whence we get the word *creed*) literally meant, "I set my heart on." Faith was an activity that involved the center of our entire being, not merely our brain cells. In the early creeds, *credo* did include the mind's acceptance of certain precepts, but these were not the objects of faith. It was God in whom the Christians placed their trust and allegiance, not words or sentences. Faith consisted of a dynamic interplay between mental activity and practical activity, belief and trust, conviction and allegiance, confidence and loyalty.

In the Enlightenment of the seventeenth and eighteenth centuries, however, belief as a distinctly mental activity began increasingly to take over the activity of faith. "Belief *that* God" began to
override "belief *in* God." In fact, belief and faith have now become
virtually synonymous. But they are not synonyms, and we danger-
ously distort the meaning of *faith* when we reduce it to *belief.*

The English language has certainly not been a friend at this
point. We have no good verbal counterpart to the noun *faith.* Typically, in English, when we want to turn a noun into a verb, we
merely take the root word and add endings (such as *-es, -ing,* or *-ed*).
The noun *dance* can become the verb *dancing.* The noun *fight* can
become the verbs *fighting* or *fights.* The noun *box* can become the
verbs *boxed* or *boxing.* In all of these the root remains basically the
same while endings are added. But what about the noun *faith?* We
have no corresponding verbal form that retains the root *faith* and
simply adds endings, thereby giving it an active and verbal sense.
Think how strange it would be to use phrases such as "we faithed,"
"she is faithing," or "he faiths"! What do we do instead? Typically
we change the entire root of the word to *believe,* and in so doing we
are left with tragic consequences. *Faith,* a dynamic noun that has
both mental and practical dimensions, is reduced to a purely mental
activity—*belief*—thereby altering and severely restricting the meaning
of faith. We could, of course, create a new vocabulary. We could ask
each other about our "faithing"! Such language is probably unlikely to catch on, but it would help us to understand that faith is
always a combination of believing and acting—together. When these
get divorced, we get a distorted faith—or even, as James says, a dead
faith (2:17). Faith and belief are *not* synonyms, and the difference
between the two is critically important as we examine the various
claims of the Apostles' Creed. Christian faith can never be reduced
to a matter of merely "believing" certain propositions, doctrines, or
creeds without great damage to faith itself. Faith as a way of living
and acting may presuppose certain beliefs, but it certainly cannot be
reduced to them. Faith is loyalty.

Actually, this important distinction is not completely lost in the
film *Contact.* Most viewers (even Christians) will find themselves
identifying with Ellie more than with any other character. Despite
the fact that she can find no good reason to believe in God, she is

nonetheless, in general, a person of integrity. She is honest. David Drumlin, the film's national science advisor, on the other hand, confesses belief in God, but we don't really identify with him because he is manipulative and self-serving. Palmer Joss claims to be a man of faith, but we can't figure out what that actually means for how he lives.

It seems we know almost intuitively that belief is not at all the same thing as faith—that merely saying "I believe" does not mean a person is "faithful." Faith entails a way of living. It entails specific allegiances, commitments, and life practices. We don't really see these in the film's characters who claim to believe, and so their faith comes off as vacuous, sentimental, or even hypocritical. Ironically, it is Ellie, who does not believe, who is often the most "faith"-ful of all the characters!

Another point where this film can be helpful is in teaching us something about the uneasy relationship of faith and science in our world. A faith that tries to achieve for its claims the certainty of science is as doomed as a science that pretends it begins with no faith claims of its own. There is a yearning in our world today for a spirituality that can resolve the tensions between faith and science with integrity and practicality. Perhaps *Contact* is ultimately unsatisfying in pointing the way to such an integral spirituality, but it at least has the courage to try to imagine its possibility. Whether and how we decide to rise to that challenge is up to us. In a secular and scientific world that less and less requires religious answers, our task as Christians is to communicate a faith that is pervasive, relevant, and meaningful rather than obscure, trivial, and silly. And perhaps the one point where that task will be most difficult but most important is, as the film itself suggests, at the intersection of the human spirit and technology.

As a general uneasiness about where our technocentric world is headed becomes increasingly widespread, along with alteration after alteration in our understanding of the cosmos, we can expect more films to reflect our cosmic anxieties and the implications of those anxieties for religious faith. Christian faith cannot afford to run from those anxieties or their implications by retreating into a private world of abstract and pious *beliefs*. As we shall see in the following chapters, to say "I believe" is costly and downright revolutionary in our world. It entails a way of life that requires discipline and practice. To believe is to make a leap—not only of the mind, but of the heart, soul, and body.

QUESTIONS FOR DISCUSSION

1. What is faith? How do the two main characters in *Contact* use the word?
2. Is faith compatible with science? Are there points where the two necessarily clash? Are there any problems with a scientist's also being a Christian?
3. What examples of "religion" or "religious faith" do you see in the film? Does the film do a good job of portraying religious faith?
4. What, if anything, did you like most about the film? What, if anything, bothered you about the film? Are you left with any questions?

RELATED FILMS

At Play in the Fields of the Lord (1991)
Black Robe (1991)
Chariots of Fire (1981)
City Slickers (1991)
Dead Man Walking (1995)
Leap of Faith (1992)
A Man for All Seasons (1966)
The Mission (1986)
The Seventh Seal (1957)

NOTES

[1] This chapter was originally published in slightly different form as "Religious Faith and Science in *Contact*," *The Journal of Religion and Film* 2, no. 2 (Fall 1998), and is used with permission.
[2] Roger Ebert, *Chicago Sun-Times*, July 11, 1997.

2

"God, the Father almighty"

 *Oh, God!*

Every now and then, God plays a leading role in the movies, even when absent from the screen. In fact, some of the most important films about God are those where God's very existence is in question, such as Ingmar Bergman's classic *The Seventh Seal* (1957) or Woody Allen's *Crimes and Misdemeanors* (1989). There are films, of course, in which God, though off-screen, is assumed to be present and even drives the narrative wheels of the story. In *Amadeus* (1984), for example, composer Salieri devotes his life in service to God, but finally wages war with God and commits himself to the destruction of God's incarnation in the form of Mozart. In *The Color Purple* (1985), Celie narrates each step of her story as if it were a letter, "Dear God…," and it is this device that provides the entire framework for understanding the plot and for connecting the viewer with her perspective and pathos. Other films, such as *The Rapture* (1991) or *Breaking the Waves* (1996), feature relationships between the main characters and God that are much more direct, personal, and dramatic.

In a few films we actually get to hear God's voice. From the lavishly epic *The Ten Commandments* (1956) to the insanely ludicrous *Monty Python and the Holy Grail* (1975),[1] God's thundering voice has helped to inspire awe and even to make us laugh—especially when the voice of God is recognizably that of a familiar actor. Gene Hackman has had the distinct honor of providing God's voice in two different movies, *Two of a Kind* (1983) and *The Next Voice You Hear* (1950).

Then there are those films in which God actually shows up on screen. God has been played by Rex Ingram (*Green Pastures*, 1936), Richard Pryor (*In God We Tru$t*, 1980), Charlton Heston (*Almost an Angel*, 1990), and even Alanis Morissette (*Dogma*, 1999). But perhaps God's most famous big-screen appearance is in Carl Reiner's *Oh, God!* (1977), a comedy that asks what might happen if the Almighty were to show up looking something like George Burns.

Oh, God!: © Warner Bros. Inc., Courtesy MoMA

God also reappears in the ever weaker sequels, *Oh, God!, Book II* (1980) and *Oh, God! You Devil* (1984).

From the very beginning of *Oh, God!* we know we are in for a nontraditional glimpse of God. Mild-mannered supermarket manager Jerry Landers (John Denver) receives a letter from God stating simply, "God grants you an interveiw." Landers puzzles over why God would misspell the word "interview," and it becomes immediately clear that we are not in the presence of the ultimate reality and absolute perfection envisioned by philosophers and theologians throughout the centuries. Indeed, this deity is much more human than most of us would expect and prefer. God confides to Landers that he has a few misgivings about some of his creations: "Tobacco was one of my big mistakes; ostriches were a mistake, silly looking things; avocados—made the pit too big. Like I say, you try!" At another point God reconsiders shame. "That was another little goof of mine—shame. I don't know why I thought we needed shame."

The film does not throw out God's supreme power and transcendence altogether, however. God's incarnation in the form of a kindly old grandfather in a baseball cap is for our benefit. Says God, "I don't like to brag, but if I appeared to you just as God, how I really am, what I really am, your mind couldn't grasp it." Clearly, God is a God with extraordinary power. He can make it rain in Landers' automobile (a Pacer), and he can appear and disappear at will. God can even make his voice come out of a car radio. But even though God does admit to performing miracles every now and then (the '69 Mets), they are certainly not his modus operandi; he sees them as too flashy and disruptive of the natural balance. "I'm not sure how this whole miracle business got started, the idea that anything connected with me has to be a miracle. Personally, I'm sorry that it did. It makes the distance between us even greater."

Carl Reiner's version of God is a downsized deity who avoids doing for humans what they can do for themselves. God is no cosmic micromanager with an answer for everything and an infallible plan for each being on the planet. When asked by Landers if he listens to us, God replies, "I can't help hearing. I don't always listen." Landers becomes frustrated by the fact that people do not believe he has actually had an encounter with God and presses God for more details about his plan, only to find out that God is concerned primarily with the big picture: "I don't get into details." Asked whether he has at least some kind of scheme, God replies, "A lot of it is luck. I gave you a world and everything in it. The rest is up to you." When Landers exclaims, "But you know everything!" the Almighty retorts, "I only know what is. Also I'm very big on what was. On what isn't yet, I haven't got a clue. People have to decide on their own what's to be done with the world. I can't make a personal decision for everybody."

Despite the fact that God is not personally involved in every detail of the world, there are nonetheless signs of his care and concern—for example, his initiative in choosing Landers to carry his message of hope and encouragement to the world. And yet, even here it's difficult not to conclude that everything happens pretty much by chance. When Landers asks, "Why me?" God responds, "Why not you? Life is a crapshoot, like the millionth customer who crosses the bridge gets to shake hands with the governor. You're better than some, not as good as others, but you crossed the bridge at the right time."

As the film unfolds, Landers has the difficult assignment of trying to convince the world that he has had an encounter with God. He can't help but look foolish and even insane to the religious news editor of the *Los Angeles Times,* and he is made to look ridiculous on *Dinah Shore*, a popular television talk show of the 1970s. He especially meets resistance from leaders of the local religious community who question the authenticity of his encounter. His wife, played by Teri Garr, likewise has a hard time swallowing the news. Coincidentally, Garr plays the wife of another man visited by an extraterrestrial being in *Close Encounters of the Third Kind*, a film also released in 1977.

Many Christians will undoubtedly have difficulties with several aspects of God's portrayal in this film. *Oh, God!* calls into question at least two of the qualities classically associated with God— omniscience (supreme knowledge) and omnipotence (supreme power). Christians with a strong sense of God's providence and plan for their lives will find this especially annoying, and some may even see it as blasphemous. Also, there are points where the writers have God make comments that contradict the Bible—though typically for the sake of humor and not at all as an attack on the Bible itself. About the act of creation, for example, God confides that it actually didn't take him six days to create the world at all—instead, he thought about it for five days and did the whole job in one. Responding to the question of whether there will actually be a judgment day, God surmises, "If they mean a doomsday, an end of the world, I'm certainly not going to get into that. But if you want my personal opinion, I wouldn't look forward to it. There'd be a lot of yelling and screaming, and I don't need that any more than you do."

An important segment of the film with which a number of Christians will be the most uncomfortable is God's answer to the question of whether Jesus Christ is the Son of God: "Jesus was my son. Buddha was my son. Mohammed, Moses, you, the man who said there was no room in the inn…" The deity of *Oh, God!* clearly wants to be the God of all creatures and refuses to be owned by any one particular religious tradition—or, for that matter, by religion itself. When Landers mentions that he has read an article that claims religion is on the upswing, God remarks, "Religion is easy. I'm talking about faith." And when Landers asks why God would choose him as a messenger, given the fact that Landers belongs to no church, God replies, "Neither do I."

From the standpoint of traditional Christian teaching, it is easy to find fault with Reiner's portrayal of God—in that respect, the film is a slow-moving target. As we examine the creed's affirmation of God through the lens of this film, however, and as we compare and contrast the George Burns version of God with the God of the creed, we would do well to remember that we are dealing here with two completely different genres of human expression.[2] It would be difficult enough to dramatize on screen a subject as complex and impenetrable as God—especially in a way that is balanced, consistent, and respectful. Add to that the fact that comedy as a genre does not even intend to offer balance, fairness, and respect. Hyperbole, irony, and sarcasm are its stock-in-trade. Distortion and irreverence are essential to its purpose. If this film is helpful at all as a partner in theological dialogue, it will not be so much because it offers us a serious constructive proposal for envisioning the Divine Being, but rather because, through spoof and satire, it challenges us and helps us rethink our own notions about who God is.

God, the "Father almighty"

The Apostles' Creed uses two phrases to speak of God. The first is "Father almighty," and the second is "Creator of heaven and earth." In this chapter we will explore the first of these by reflecting on Carl Reiner's version of God. Whether the character played by George Burns is anything at all like the "Father almighty" of the creed depends, of course, on how we understand these two important words.

First of all, let us admit that there is a danger in speaking about God as *Father*. The temptation is to begin with prior assumptions about fatherhood and then to impose those assumptions uncritically upon our idea of God. Some of these assumptions are not at all Christian and have taken shape in cultures that are predominantly patriarchal, where the roles of men and women have been defined by age-old patterns of subordination and domination. In addition, many of our assumptions about fatherhood have been deeply informed by our own experiences of our earthly fathers. These experiences can be helpful in grasping the Christian vision of God as father, but they can also be major obstacles. While Jesus can compare human parents to the fatherhood of God (Mt. 7:9–11), it is nonetheless clear that our parenting pales in comparison to God's parenting.

Christians, therefore, must exercise caution in talking about God as *Father*. We do not begin with our culture's general understanding of fatherhood and then proceed toward thinking about God. Rather, we travel the opposite route. We learn the proper meaning of fatherhood by watching and imitating God the Father. And for Christians, the source for understanding God as *the Father* is Jesus *the Son*. When we talk about God as Father, we are not speaking philosophically of some abstract point of origin, nor psychologically of a supreme wish-fulfiller, nor even are we speaking sociologically of an authoritarian source behind the status quo. Instead, we begin concretely with Jesus of Nazareth and the Father whom he talked about and revealed. Thus, despite the fact that Jesus is not mentioned explicitly in the creed until the second major section, already in the first words of the creed Christians affirm that all our talk of God finds its starting point in him. Thus, "to speak of God as Father is to speak already of Jesus, for it is in and through Jesus that we are able to speak of God as Father."[3]

When we look at how Jesus himself actually used the word *Father* to speak of God, one of the first things that strikes us is the way Jesus integrates and blends what are generally considered to be masculine and paternal qualities with what are generally considered to be feminine and maternal qualities. From the standpoint of the New Testament, it is impossible to make a list of stereotypical patriarchal qualities in one column and a list of stereotypical matriarchal qualities in another column and then place God in the first. A study of the four gospels reveals that Jesus consistently understands the fatherhood of God in a way that breaks out of the standard patriarchal framework. Not one of the four gospels has Jesus using the word *Father* in the context of judgment or wrath. Jesus is never found using the term to portray legal demand, justice, hierarchical authority, or emotional distance. All of this does not mean that Jesus does not conceive of God as a God who makes demands— a God of justice, or even wrath. The point is, however, that it is not these kinds of qualities that Jesus associates with the word *Father*. Instead, the Father is the one who "gives good things to his children" (Mt. 7:11; Lk. 11:13) and "to those who ask him" (Mt. 6:6, 32). The Father rewards his children and takes care of them just as surely as he cares for the birds (Mt. 6:26). The Father is forgiving (Mt. 6:14; Mk. 11:25) and merciful (Lk. 6:36), benevolent both to the evil and the good, the righteous and the unrighteous (Mt. 5:45). In fact, one of the most important characteristics of *Father*, as Jesus uses the word, is that it is not so much a form of theological description as it is a form of intimate personal address. God is not simply "the Father." God is *our* Father—or, as Jesus himself says, "Daddy" (*abba*).

What this means, according to Jesus, is that a conversion must take place to understanding ourselves as God's children (Mt. 18:3–6). To live a life that is loyal to God the Father is to live life creatively, but receptively, in both confidence and humility. The *kingdom of God*—that state in which God's will is accomplished—is no longer a remote possibility for those who are children of God, "for your Father has chosen gladly to give you the kingdom" (Lk. 12:32).

Like the prodigal who returns to his father, there are no hoops through which we must jump, no scratching and clawing to earn approval or win respect. To say "I believe in God the Father" is to confess that God has granted to us full and free participation in the family of God—the only condition being our willingness to turn around and head home.

The second term used to describe God in the creed is *almighty*, and like the word *Father*, we should exercise caution in how we use it to describe God. Jesus himself never uses the word, though it can be found with frequency in the Old Testament and rarely in the New Testament.[4] The difficulty with using a word such as *almighty* without some qualification is that the whole notion of power as applied to God has been turned on its head and revolutionized in the person of Jesus. Given the meaning we tend to attach to such a term, using it to refer to God may actually cause us to say the very opposite of what Jesus taught about God.

Like fatherhood, God's character as *almighty* must not be viewed in the abstract as sheer power, sovereignty, or force. The word *almighty* in the creed is not a noun, as in the case of *Father*. It is an adjective used to modify *Father*. When the creed claims God is *almighty*, it is in the context of God's role as Father. God is the one who is almighty to give and forgive, the one who is powerful enough to provide and care for us. God is not some impersonal supreme force in the universe, but the supreme lover, liberator, and nurturer of God's children. We cannot simply start with our standard definition of what it would mean to be omnipotent or almighty and then apply it to God the Father. According to the apostle Paul, the power of God appears as foolishness to the worldly-wise, and it is most perfectly expressed in Jesus hanging on a cross (1 Cor. 1:24). Now, to the eyes of the world, crucifixion does not look very much like power, but weakness. Nor is Christ's unpretentious birth in a manger or life among the poor and outcast an especially prominent display of strength or might, at least by the world's standards. Power is utterly redefined in the New Testament. Even in the book of Revelation, the conquering lion of Judah—the one who has overcome and is alone worthy and able to break the seven seals—turns out to be…a lamb (Rev. 5:1–6). If Christ is the final and decisive revelation of who God is, then Christians must hold that divine power is the

power to love, persuade, and forgive rather than the power to dominate, coerce, and bend to the will of another. It is a power born of
intimacy and solidarity, not a remote power dropped in from above.

Returning to the unassuming and down-to-earth deity of *Oh,
God!*, is it possible to find in this film something of a parallel to the
surprising—even shocking—humility of the God who "became
flesh" and "dwelt among us" (Jn. 1:14)? There is something refreshing and disarming about the way Carl Reiner's version of God
challenges and undermines the stereotypically macho, supreme-ruler-
of-the-universe versions of God that are so tied up with patriarchy
and non-Christian mythology—the old, bearded man of
Michelangelo in the Sistine Chapel. The divine being of *Oh, God!*
is not a stern, authoritarian lawgiver or judge. He is relaxed, non-
threatening, and generally nonjudgmental (although he does suggest that a local evangelist be instructed to "sell shoes and shut up").
In the film's closing court scene, when Jerry Landers is being ques-
tioned by an attorney about the authenticity of his encounter with
God, we find the following exchange:

> "And the Absolute Being, the All-Powerful, All-Merciful,
> the All-Knowing Infinite Spirit, the Supreme Soul, the King
> of Kings and Lord of Lords, the Infinite, Everlasting, Eternal
> Being last came to you *how?*"
>
> "As a bellhop."
>
> "Your honor, I rest my case!"

The notion that God would appear as a bellhop is hysterical, and
laughter fills the courtroom. But is it any less ridiculous to believe
that God was born in a manger or suffered cruelly on a cross? In a
number of ways that resemble the on-screen version of God, the
Father of Jesus of Nazareth defies our expectations and stereotypes.

Yet, from a Christian perspective, there is still something
important missing in the deity incarnate in the form of George
Burns. God the *Father* has been replaced by God the *Grandfather*—
a harmless old codger with spunk but no fire and wit but no bite.
Popular-movie–going audiences may well be drawn to the idea of
a kindly old God who is no longer the booming voice speaking to
Charlton Heston in *The Ten Commandments* or the manipulative

supreme being of *The Wizard of Oz*. But is this really a God with substance—a God who cares about us deeply and about whom we should care deeply?

Andrew Greeley, in a study of God and God-images in American film, concludes that what is ultimately missing in these portrayals taken as a whole is a sense of divine justice and outrage. Instead God's mercy and compassion are given more prominence:

> Movies…tell us that American religion is firmly committed to the notion of a gracious rather than a punitive God, perhaps because America is a nation dedicated to freedom and a nation that never suffered too much (not since the Civil War, anyway) and Americans are incorrigible optimists. God in the movies is someone who supports and sustains American optimism.[5]

Greeley is probably right, but in the case of *Oh, God!* it is not only God's punitive side that is missing; ultimately, God's mercy and compassion are missing as well. Reiner's version of God is unlike Jesus' *Father* not primarily because this God is not judgmental, demanding, or punitive enough. Rather, it is because this God is not intimate, caring, and loving enough. In Jesus, we discover that it is these latter qualities that provide the starting point for understanding the former, not vice-versa. It is possible to talk about God in such a way as to insist on a balance between God's compassion and justice as if they were two fundamentally different qualities that must be held together like two ends of a seesaw. We might do better, however, to view them more like two sides of one coin—with the one coin being love (1 Jn. 4:8, 16). God is the God who knows us and loves us, who has entered into solidarity with us and is intimate with us. From this intimacy flow both compassion and justice, both forgiveness and anger. Is it really possible to watch *Oh, God!* and conclude that this God *loves* us? Just because God is a simple, down-to-earth old man does not mean God actually cares. It is possible, after all, to be nonjudgmental and, at the same time, fail to be intimate or involved. The real problem with the George Burns version of God is not that he is too anthropomorphic—too bereft of classical divine qualities such as omnipotence, omniscience, or supernatural transcendence—but that he just doesn't seem to care all that much, nor does it seem plausible that we should really care about him. Film critic Pauline Kael notes that the picture is so overly cautious about not offending anyone that it ends up with "a greeting-card shallowness," embodied in phrases like "Give brotherly love a chance." According to Kael, "listening to God's bland messages...is like sinking in a mountain of white flour."[6]

Reiner seems concerned that God not be perceived as a cosmic crutch, an overbearing and infinite giant who predestines all that happens, thereby reducing humans to the role of pawns or puppets. Undoubtedly this is a healthy corrective to distorted versions of God that pay for his sovereignty at the expense of human freedom. Reiner, however, leaves unanswered what exactly God's role is in our world and in our lives—why should we be interested in God? The God incarnate in the form of George Burns will neither be responsible for fixing the world for us nor held accountable for the suffering and the evil in our world. Everything is up to us. That may be all well and good, but it is difficult then to figure out what the difference is between believing in such a God and finally concluding that we are alone in the universe. In fact, God even refuses to be the source of life's meaning. Human existence "means exactly and precisely not more, not one tiny bit less, just what you think it means, and what I think doesn't count at all," says George Burns.

In the end, the deity of *Oh, God!* is still utterly patriarchal—only not now the stern taskmaster and lawgiver, but the detached old grandfather. What is still missing is compassion and justice that are both born equally out of solidarity and intimacy. God is still the aloof patriarch—the one who gives us a world and then tells us to pull ourselves up by our own bootstraps. And "almighty" is still reduced to appearing, vanishing, and reappearing, doing card tricks, speaking out of car radios, and making it rain inside a car. Christianity envisions a God who doesn't do everything for us, to be sure, but who is nonetheless the gracious source of our lives and our love—a God who is almighty, not in the sense of capricious or whimsical power, but in the sense of gracious "reliability" (Ps. 19:7–10).

Believing in God

As we saw in the previous chapter, when Christians say, "I believe in God, the Father almighty," they are talking about much more than an intellectual exercise. Perhaps the creed would be better translated, "I *trust* in God, the Father almighty" or "I am *loyal* to God, the Father almighty." Faith includes central convictions about the nature of God, but faith is also an intensely practical activity expressed in specific allegiances, life commitments, and daily routines—the way we acquire possessions and consume the world's resources, how and for whom we work, our commitment to the poor, diseased, elderly, and victimized, the way we treat our family members, neighbors, and enemies. To say we believe in God is much more than raw belief in a supernatural being who rules the universe. As a Christian, to believe in God, the Father almighty is to live as if there *is* a God who *is* the Father almighty.

It may be helpful at this point to distinguish between a theoretical atheist and a practical atheist. A theoretical atheist is a person who does not believe there is a God. A practical atheist, however, is one who lives as if there is no God, regardless of whether God's existence is acknowledged explicitly or not. As Jesus repeatedly emphasized, it is possible to affirm God's existence with our minds and with our mouths without ever allowing that belief to transform our lives and our activity (Mt. 7:21; 25:31–46).

In *Oh, God!* we can begin to see ever so faintly the repercussions on his life, work, and family relationships of Jerry Landers' encounter with God. One of the limitations of the film, however, is that we are never really led to imagine in more than a superficial way the kind of life practice and allegiances that believing in God would yield. As we saw in the film *Contact*, belief in God is reduced to belief that God *is*—an important aspect of faith to be sure, but not at all the whole of faith or the center of faith.

To believe in God as the *almighty Father*, however, yields some concrete and practical consequences for our lives. If God is *Father*, we are invited into a community where compassion and justice are the order of the day and where all humans are valued and nurtured. If God is Father, all humans are God's children and therefore brothers and sisters. To believe in the fatherhood of God is to refuse to tolerate the marginalization or victimization of some of God's children. Loyalty to this God, therefore, means a commitment to human equality and freedom as well as an end to the forces that oppress and discriminate. It is impossible to understand oneself as a child of God the Father and continue patterns of consumption whereby a small minority of the world's population lives in affluence and comfort while the majority of the world's population lives in want and poverty. To believe in God the Father means that our wants must be shaped in accordance with the needs of others.

Likewise, to believe in God, the Father *almighty* means that we are freed from the oppressive fear and burden of trying to earn salvation or entry into God's liberation community. God is the source of that community—the bountiful giver and gracious provider of all our needs. As children of God, the *Father* we are invited to share with God in creatively building a liberation community. But as children of God, the Father *almighty*, we are freed from the anxiety and fear that come from relying on our own efforts—of calculating and adding up our deeds to see if they merit our acceptance before God and neighbor. To believe in God, the *Father almighty* means that life need no longer be lived as a test; it can be lived creatively as a project of love.

QUESTIONS FOR DISCUSSION

1. Does the film make you think about God in new ways? Does anything bother you about the George Burns version of God? Is anything about that version appealing to you?
2. The Apostles' Creed uses the phrase, "I believe in God, the Father almighty." What do we mean when we say God is "Father"?
3. What do we mean when we say God is "almighty"?
4. The portrayal of deity in *Oh, God!* undoubtedly runs contrary to many of our popular notions of God. In what ways does the Christian view of God run contrary to such popular notions?
5. What concrete difference in life, if any, does it make to believe in God?

RELATED FILMS

Breaking the Waves (1996)
Contact (1997)
Crimes and Misdemeanors (1989)

Dogma (1999)
The Seventh Seal (1957)
Star Trek V: The Final Frontier (1989)
The Wizard of Oz (1939)

NOTES

[1]In fact, God is the only character to appear in all three Monty Python films: *Monty Python and the Holy Grail* (1975), *Monty Python's Life of Brian* (1979), and *Monty Python's The Meaning of Life* (1983).

[2]Not all Christian reviewers of this film have taken adequately into account the simple fact of the film's genre as comedy and what that means for how we should interpret the film. As a result, *Oh, God!* has sometimes been attacked as a misleading and even dangerous portrayal of God, akin to heretical Gnostic works in the first century or secular humanism in the twentieth century. Such is the case with Philip A. Siddons, "'Oh, God!' Oh, Carl Reiner!" *Christianity Today* 22 (1977): 419–20.

[3]Theodore W. Jennings, Jr., *Loyalty to God: The Apostles' Creed in Life and Liturgy* (Nashville: Abingdon Press, 1992), 75.

[4]"Almighty" is found frequently in Revelation and also appears in 2 Corinthians 6:18: "'And I will be a father to you, and you shall be sons and daughters to me,' says the Lord Almighty." Paul is quoting from 2 Samuel and, interestingly, links the term "Lord Almighty" with this quotation about God's Fatherhood.

[5]Andrew M. Greeley, "Images of God in the Movies," *The Journal of Religion and Film* 1, no.1 (1997).

[6]Pauline Kael, *5001 Nights at the Movies* (Henry Holt & Company, 1990), 510.

3

"Creator of heaven and earth"

 *2001: A Space Odyssey*

Before spaceships began screaming across the big screen shooting up intergalactic villains and making the universe a safer place to live, director Stanley Kubrick managed to portray the mystery, expanse, and beauty of space in the imaginative film *2001: A Space Odyssey*. Released in 1968 (one year before the first moon landing), *2001* is still considered by many critics and fans to be unsurpassed in both its artistic vision and technical achievement. One of the great ironies of the film is that while it ultimately wants to say something about the extrodinary place of humans in the universe, humans are deliberately dwarfed in comparison to this larger purpose, and their emotions and relationships are restricted and marginalized. Even the spacecraft's onboard computer seems to have more sensitivity and passion than the astronauts on board. Perhaps it is for this reason that the film is not always perceived as "entertaining" and why it did not do well at the box office in its initial release. More than twenty minutes expire in the film before a single line of dialogue is heard, and the film concludes with close to another half-hour without dialogue.[1] Eventually, however, the film did turn out to be one of MGM Studio's top moneymakers and has since gained the status of a classic. It can regularly be found on the top-ten lists of serious critics and popular fans all over the world. At the heart of *2001* are the twin questions of an ultimate creative intelligence in the universe and the nature and destiny of human existence within this larger design.

The film begins with prehistoric apes encountering a large, black, geometrically perfect "monolith" that transforms them into beings with will and purpose who are now able to begin fashioning tools for themselves. Kubrick never offers an answer to the source of the monolith, and this has left the film open to a variety of religious and metaphysical interpretations, a situation in which Kubrick himself always reveled and did little to alter. When once asked about the meaning of the film, he replied,

> It's not a message that I ever intend to convey in words. *2001* is a nonverbal experience…I tried to create a visual experience, one that bypasses verbalized pigeonholing and directly penetrates the subconscious with an emotional and philosophic content…I intended the film to be an intensely subjective experience that reaches the viewer at an inner level of consciousness, just as music does; to "explain" a Beethoven symphony would be to emasculate it by erecting an artificial barrier between conception and appreciation. You're free to speculate as you wish about the philosophical and allegorical meaning of the film—and such speculation is one indication that it has succeeded in gripping the audience at a deep level—but I don't want to spell out a verbal road map for *2001* that every viewer will feel obligated to pursue or else fear he's missed the point.[2]

It should not be surprising, then, that for more than thirty years both trained and casual reviewers of *2001* have continued to put forward theories about its meaning. Some reviewers have seen in the film a quasi-Darwinian[3] vision of human existence in which we evolve through natural processes, but in which there are also evolutionary "leaps" induced by encounters with this transcendent power, thereby accounting for any anthropological "missing links." Other interpreters associate the film with the philosophy of Friedrich Nietzsche.[4] Certainly Kubrick's use of Richard Strauss's heart-pounding "Thus Spake Zarathustra," inspired by Nietzsche, sends a powerful message at key points in the film that humans are ascending to territory reserved only for the gods.[5]

From primeval apes the film transports us forward to the year 2001 in what has been called "the longest flash-forward in the history of cinema."[6] Human beings have advanced considerably in the kinds of tools we now use (spacecraft, two-way televisions, computers), but the dissolve from a prehistoric bone floating in the air into a satellite orbiting the earth establishes a continuity between our prehistory and our future. So also our tools retain a similar capacity both for creative and destructive purposes. In 2001 a new monolith has been discovered on the moon, deliberately buried four million years ago. The monolith emits an ear-piercing signal toward Jupiter where yet another monolith will appear as the doorway to an entirely new stage in human development. As the spacecraft approaches the monolith, the HAL-9000 onboard computer takes over, turns off the life support systems of the astronauts in hibernation, and locks out the two astronauts who have been guiding the spacecraft. One of the astronauts, Dave Bowman, finally makes his way back into the ship and manages to disconnect HAL, who seems to be experiencing some kind of nervous breakdown. In one of the most dramatic scenes in the film, Dave begins slowly to shut down HAL's memory circuits, one by one. Dave's increased breathing reveals his panic and fear. At the same time, HAL pleads for Dave not to disconnect him, and as his mind is going, his own anxiety and fear can be detected despite his soft, monotone voice: "Stop, Dave. I'm afraid."

2001: A Space Odyssey: © Turner Entertainment Co., Courtesy MoMA

An implicit theme throughout the film is the relationship between machines and their human creators and whether we end up being mastered by the very technology we create to serve us. Thus, an important part of the film is the association between creator and creation, human and machine. Still, the machinery is not mere mechanics set over against human spirit in *2001*. There is a beauty and transcendence that Kubrick gives even to the machines. The rocket ships and space stations, for example, move slowly, waltzing in time to the "Blue Danube," and HAL's voice has a soothing, even spiritual, quality to it.

Having disconnected HAL, Dave leaves the ship to explore the monolith, and from this point forward, plot and narrative give way to sheer image and sound. Kubrick is not merely making a statement about ultimate reality, he is inviting the viewer to contemplate and imagine it. In the late '60s, when the film was first released, some members of the audience would more fully participate by "tripping" during the final scenes! As Dave makes contact with the monolith, a dramatic light show develops on screen as the stars fold in around him, apparently signaling a new form of cosmic awareness. The monolith becomes a "stargate" as Dave is apparently transported to some other place or dimension in the universe. As computers and spaceships recede into the background, a new human is born— cosmically advanced (Dave grows very old) and yet reborn as a star-child, the next leap forward in human evolution.

In the end, the mystery of the universe—that which creates life and toward which all life is advancing—remains a mystery in *2001*, and appropriately so. The film elicits a sense of awe both visually and in terms of its sound editing and musical score; it combines symmetry and the psychedelic, the human and the machine, rationality and enigma.

God, the Creator of Heaven and Earth

As previously mentioned, the monolith in *2001* may be interpreted in a number of ways, none of them more "right" than the others. Interpreted through the lens of a Christian theology of creation, however, the black, impenetrable monolith becomes a symbol of God's mysterious, creative power, which has "pulled at" humans—and, indeed, at all life—from the beginning. This creative power is not merely the initial force that brought the universe into being, but that which guides the universe toward its divine purpose. One of the disastrous consequences of the way the modern debate over creation and evolution has been framed is that it has tended to reduce Christian thinking about creation to little more than a question of origins. To speak of God as Creator, however, is not only to make a statement about the past; it is also to make a statement about the present and the future. Belief in creation is fundamentally a belief about God's relationship to and involvement in the world. Furthermore, the preoccupation with building rational explanations for and defenses of how the universe actually came to be often misses the sense of poetry and mystery in creation. This can be just as true of a staunch creationist who treats the book of Genesis as if it were a scientific textbook as it is of a scientist who refuses to recognize any forces other than purely physical ones at play in the universe. Ironically, both the creationist and the evolutionist often end up playing on the same rationalistic playground, equally children of the Enlightenment and more interested in reason, logic, and explanation than beauty, story, and participation.

However one views the monolith in *2001*, though, there is no way of understanding it as merely a part of the "natural" order. Its odd perfection stands in stark contrast to everything around it. The monolith symbolizes creation as an ongoing "gift" rather than as a solely natural process. In theological terms, we can say that not only are we "saved by grace," we are "created by grace" as well. God does not simply wind up the cosmos like a watch that will run on its own, but is instead present with us, leading and luring us into the future.

There are, of course, difficulties with interpreting the monolith of *2001* as a symbol for God's creative power in the world. This big slab, while powerful and geometrically perfect, bears little resemblance to the "living God" of the Bible—the one who interacts with other living beings and to whom we make a difference. The interaction between creator and creation in *2001* is wooden and unilateral. The monolith merely appears and sits there, and though it affects us, we do not, in turn, appear to affect the monolith. The God of the Bible, on the other hand, is lively and dynamic, the one who is present with us and yet always out ahead of us, the one who enjoys and experiences us. Still, as a symbol, the monolith is effective in pointing to the reality of a creative power in our universe that calls us forward beyond ourselves and beyond our past into richer and more novel possibilities than we had ever imagined.[7]

To believe in God as Creator, then, is more than merely believing something about the past, and it is much more than a tidy explanation of the world's origins. In fact (to put it bluntly), the doctrine of creation doesn't "explain" much at all. Belief in divine creation may even create more problems than it solves. Belief in creation does, however, orient us in a new way toward God, the world, each other, and all other forms of life in the world. To affirm with the Apostles' Creed, "I believe in God, the Father almighty, creator of heaven and earth," is, first, an expression of confidence that the world is a gift from God, and therefore "good" (Gen. 1:31). It is, second, an expression of our loyalty to the giver of this good gift. If nothing else, this creation faith implies a commitment to treat creation with respect and care—to steward it. It is impossible, therefore, to be a true "creationist" and, at the same time, maintain an indifference toward the pollution of the earth or the needless injury and torment of animal life.

Furthermore, though creation itself points to God the Creator ("The heavens are telling of the glory of God; and their expanse is declaring the work of His hands"[8]), the Christian is unwilling to talk about the Creator (just as we saw in the previous chapter with the words "almighty Father") apart from Jesus of Nazareth, whom we take as our starting point in all talk about God. To exercise faith in God, the Father almighty as Creator is to affirm that the universe bears the indelible impression of and is being lovingly guided by the Father of Jesus of Nazareth. Thus, when John says, "All things came into being by [the Word], and apart from [the Word] nothing came into being that has come into being" (Jn. 1:3), and when Paul says, "all things have been created by [Christ] and for [Christ]" (Col. 1:16), we are not being handed an explanation of how the world was created. Both John and Paul are claiming that the same purpose that is incarnate in Jesus Christ is at the heart of our universe. Our universe "bends," so to speak, toward Christ. It is in this sense that Christ as alpha is also omega, the beginning and the end.[9] Just as Christ is loving and compassionate, so the universe bends toward love and compassion. Just as Christ is just, so also the universe bends toward justice.

A creation faith, therefore, leaves plenty of room for mystery and, it should be added, plenty of room for science. There is much about the world and its origins that a Christian belief in creation simply does not pretend to answer. Whatever course of events by which the world came into being—gradually over millions of years, or in a sudden creative leap or leaps—a creation faith begins with loyalty to Jesus of Nazareth, our central clue for understanding God as the source of the universe.[10]

Created in the Image of God

To refer to God as Creator, then, is not only to say something important about God; ultimately it is to say something important about creation and, specifically, about God's human creations. In the case of humans, however, our creation carries with it unique opportunities and challenges. We must ask what it means to be created "in God's image" (Gen. 1:27).

If we look at the Genesis creation story for clues to understanding our creation in the image of God, we find that several of God's characteristics are characteristics human beings also share, even if in a radically limited and derivative sense. One of those is *freedom*. Just as Adam and Eve were capable of making their world into whatever they wanted, so we also are intended for freedom. Our freedom has its limits whereas God's does not, but the possibilities for self-fulfillment and for living in harmony with each other and with nature are vast. A second characteristic whereby we reflect God's image is our creation in *community*, including our ability to love. In the Genesis 1 version of the creation story, the male and female are created together in God's image. In the Genesis 2 version, God creates the man first and then says, "It is not good for the man to be alone" (2:18). In both versions, community is deeply rooted in us as human beings and reflective of a God who is also social. As 1 John 4:8 puts it, "God is love."

The third and perhaps most important way in which we are created in God's image is through *creativity* itself. It is our capacity for reflecting divine creativity that renders our freedom more than merely having choices and that renders our community more than merely being related to others. "Creativity is the element of novelty in each of our lives whereby we receive from our past and from those influences around us, and then freely determine a future for ourselves and for our world. Thus, creativity is a function of both community and freedom. Indeed, it is the lively interplay between the two."[11] It is our reflection of God's creativity that allows us not only to *live* life but to *lead* it.

Interestingly, it is this third quality, creativity, that *2001* emphasizes most powerfully. Prior to the appearance of the monolith, the apes are barely surviving, lacking the strength to hold their own ground and steadily diminishing in numbers due to attacks from other beasts. The monolith, however, transforms the apes into creative beings—beings who are able to transcend their own creaturely limitations and the harshness of their environment by construction of basic tools and, in time, advanced technologies.[12] In the act of creation, we are called to become cocreators with God and then given that creative capacity by God. Even in the garden of Eden, God commands Adam and Eve to "be fruitful and multiply" and to work and cultivate the garden. We are summoned by God to create both through work and through love.

The most profound yet enigmatic expression of this cocreativity in *2001* is to be found in its ending as Dave Bowman is transformed into the "star-child." It would seem at this point that Dave has become at least semi-divine and is granted a celestial view of the world with incomprehensible power and intelligence. Kubrick has here allowed his imagination to run wild, and the Christian viewer may finally decide that the line between creator and creature has become far too blurred in the film. Perhaps what we see on screen is the ultimate expression of human pride and the original sin, the desire to be like God or at least the Nietzschean approximation, the superman. Of course, one could argue that we humans have been created in God's image, and so perhaps *2001* only points the way forward imaginatively (and radically) along a path that was begun long ago in the garden of Eden—the path of cocreation with God. Still, one has to consider carefully whether Dave's divinization on the scale imagined in *2001* is ultimately a helpful or harmful symbol for expressing the kind of cocreation with God toward which the Bible points.

The point here is that human creativity is a double-edged sword. The same creativity that allows us to transcend our creaturely limitations can also lead to pride and arrogance. In fact, as in *2001*, while our technological creations move us forward, they also threaten to destroy us. It is in this respect that a simple bone in the hands of a would-be human comes to define the human condition.[13] The same tools that we creatively fashion as beings who *reflect* God's image can also be used to *distort* and *corrupt* that image through slavery, exploitation, and ultimately murder.

The HAL-9000 computer in *2001* plays an important symbolic role in this respect. HAL represents the effort of created beings to reach perfection through technological advancement, albeit by finally forgetting their own creator and ultimately subordinating the creator to their own plans and purposes. HAL refers to himself as "the most reliable computer ever made" and "foolproof and incapable of error." His obsession with accuracy and perfection, however, ends up costing the lives of all but one of the crew members.

For those familiar with Kubrick's other films,[14] his vision of the fallenness of creation will come as no surprise. As James Wall says,

> Kubrick's vision of human nature is bleak…But there is an irony in this assertion since Kubrick makes this point through a medium that is remarkable for its creative achievement, and he presents his personal vision in a manner that celebrates creativity itself. The bleakness comes, therefore, from Kubrick's belief that creativity is tainted at the center…In religious language, Kubrick is presenting his conviction that "sin" is a part of the human condition and of all that is touched by human creativity.[15]

Thus, while Kubrick celebrates the technology that humans have developed to transcend their creaturely conditions, "he uses the same technology to underscore the vacuity of his characters."[16] In *2001*, humans have so come to depend on their machines they often appear on their way to becoming machines themselves. Consider, for example, the hollow conversations that occur in *2001*—the trivial exchanges and meaningless chit-chat, the superficiality of how Dr. Heywood Floyd and the scientists at Clavius moonbase patronize one another. The humans of *2001* can create elaborate ships that can fly to Jupiter, but apparently they no longer have anything of importance to say to one another on a personal level. On the flight to Jupiter, Dave and Frank sit next to each other eating their dinners almost robotically, never uttering a word, merely staring at their own individual monitors.

Interpreted through a Christian lens, *2001* asks us to consider the possibility of a mysterious, creative presence in the universe that calls us forward beyond what we think imaginable. Its gift to us is a capacity for becoming increasingly human and, therefore, increasingly reflective of the image of God. With this gift comes a warning, however. When we forget the creator, when we turn in on ourselves and on our own tools and abilities, the very creativity that generates authentic freedom and community can become destructive and stagnant as we end up serving our technology rather than allowing it to serve us.

QUESTIONS FOR DISCUSSION

1. Do you think there is an overarching message or purpose in this film? Is there some vision or statement that you think the director is attempting to communicate?
2. Discuss the religious implications, if any, that you see in the film. What do you make of the black monolith? Does it have any religious symbolism?
3. What observations do you make with regard to the role of the human beings in the film—their relationships to one another and their relationships to their technology?
4. What does it mean for humans to be created in "the image of God"?

RELATED FILMS

2010 (1984)
Altered States (1980)
Blade Runner (1982)
Earth (1930)
The Hellstrom Chronicle (1971)
Inherit the Wind (1960)
Koyaanisqatsi (1983)
Mindwalk (1991)

NOTES

[1]In fact, there are less than forty total minutes of dialogue out of two hours and nineteen minutes of film.

[2]Quoted in Jerome Agel, ed., *The Making of Kubrick's* 2001 (New York: Signet, 1970).

[3]Peter Hasenberg, "The 'Religious' in Film: From *King of Kings* to *The Fisher King*," in *New Image of Religious Film*, ed. John R. May, (Kansas City: Sheed & Ward, 1997), 49.

[4]Friedrich Nietzsche (1844–1900) was an influential atheistic philosopher famous for his oft-quoted phrase, "God is dead." Nietzsche believed the "will to power" was the basic human motive, and through his criticisms of conventional morality he sought to make room in the world for a higher form of humanity that would rise above the culture of the masses and the virtues of mediocrity that he believed were enshrined in Christianity and Western civilization.

[5]Roger Ebert, *Chicago Sun-Times,* April 8, 1968.

[6]Ibid.

[7]Cf. John Cobb, *God and the World* (Philadelphia: Westminster Press, 1969), 42–66.

[8]See Psalm 19:1–6; cf. Psalm 8:1–3 and Romans 1:20.

[9]Cf. the work of Pierre Teilhard de Chardin, whose writings consistently develop this important thesis, especially *Science and Christ*, translated by René Hague (New York: Harper & Row, 1968).

[10]See Colossians 1:15–17.

[11]Bryan P. Stone, *Compassionate Ministry: Theological Foundations* (Maryknoll, N.Y.: Orbis Books, 1996), 34.

[12]It may be significant that the monolith is clearly absent when the apes become carnivorous and begin to use bones as weapons.

[13]James M. Wall, "*2001: A Space Odyssey* and the Search for a Center," in *Image & Likeness: Religious Visions in American Film Classics*, ed. John R. May (New York: Paulist Press, 1992), 43.

[14]For example, *Lolita* (1962), *Dr. Strangelove or: How I Learned to Stop Worrying and Love the Bomb* (1964), *A Clockwork Orange* (1971), *The Shining* (1980), *Full Metal Jacket* (1987), and *Eyes Wide Shut* (1999).

[15]Wall, 43–45.

[16]Ibid., 43.

4

"Jesus Christ, his only Son, our Lord"

 *Jesus of Montreal*

At the heart of Christianity stands a person, Jesus of Nazareth. It is this person who is the focus of the second and longest section of the Apostles' Creed, to which we now turn our attention. Since the beginning of the Christian movement, Jesus has been represented in a wide variety of artistic forms. Not surprisingly, the cinema has also served as an important vehicle for the creation and propagation of Jesus images. In fact, many of the earliest films ever made were films about Jesus. The cinema was barely two years old in 1897 when the first film about Jesus, based on his passion, was released.[1] Another film, *The Passion Play of Oberammergau*, appeared a year later and was one of the first attempts at creating a fictionalized version of a historical event in film, thereby making it something of a cinematic landmark.[2] More than a dozen other films based on the life of Christ were produced during the silent film era, and more than a hundred such films have been created throughout the entire history of the cinema. Indeed, Jesus may be the most filmed subject in history.[3]

Of course, not all films about Jesus share the same structure or approach. Some attempt to retell Jesus' life based more or less literally on the gospel accounts of the New Testament. They may vary in style, orthodoxy, reverence, and perspective, but insofar as they all attempt to express the significance of Jesus through an explicit retelling of his life, they form a class of film known as the "Jesus film."[4] Many of the early silent films about Jesus belong to this genre, as do the famous Hollywood epics such as *King of Kings* (1961) and *The Greatest Story Ever Told* (1965). A number of Jesus films created controversy when released and have even been considered by some as blasphemous. Examples range from Martin Scorsese's *The Last Temptation of Christ* (1988) to two rock-musical versions that appeared in 1973: *Godspell* and *Jesus Christ Superstar.* Still, these films can be considered "Jesus films" in that they attempt to interpret the significance of Jesus by delivering the story of his life to us on screen—despite their divergences from the literal text of the gospels. Other recent Jesus films include Roberto Rosellini's classic *The Messiah* (1975) and Franco Zeffirelli's television miniseries *Jesus of Nazareth* (1977). A motion picture that many consider to be the most artistic of the Jesus-film genre, *The Gospel According to Saint Matthew* (1966), was the creation of a Marxist director, Pier Paulo Pasolini, who fell in love with Jesus' revolutionary qualities by reading the gospel of Matthew. This film was the first to use a single gospel and only the text of that gospel for its entire narrative.

In film, as in other art forms, it is also possible to express the significance of Christ without a direct or literal telling of his life story. The meaning of Christ may instead be portrayed figuratively, as in a parable, through the use of a "Christ figure." In this case, Jesus may not even be mentioned explicitly at all in the film. On one level, the story being conveyed may be about something altogether different than the life of Jesus—it is simply a story about some slice of human life, history, experience, or imagination. On another level, however, when approached metaphorically, the film can be understood in a christological sense. It then provides an additional (and sometimes unintentional) dimension to the film, while at the same time adding texture to our understanding of the meaning of Christ for us. So, for example, the explicit story may be about an alien as in *E. T. The Extra-Terrestrial* (1982), a prisoner as in *Cool Hand Luke* (1967), a thirteenth-century Scottish warrior as in *Braveheart* (1995), or a convict in a mental institution as in *One Flew Over the Cuckoo's Nest* (1975). Implicitly, however, each of these films features a character who identifies with Christ in some way (e.g., his role as redeemer, his relationship to violence and suffering, or his death at the hands of injustice and intolerance). Jesus himself uses a Christ-figure by comparing himself to Jonah: "For just as Jonah was three days and three nights in the belly of the sea monster, so shall the Son of Man be three days and three nights in the heart of the earth" (Mt. 12:40–41).

We can also find the use of Christ-figures elsewhere in the New Testament in references to Moses or the "suffering servant" of Isaiah. Even the church is a figure that represents Christ insofar as the church is "Christ's body." Films that use a Christ-figure need not be explicitly religious; indeed, many of them are not. They are sometimes the creation of filmmakers and actors who are Christians, but they also appear in films by artists who do not claim to be believers and may even be professed atheists. Ultimately, the ability of a particular character to serve as a Christ-figure depends on the extent to which the meaning of Christ has already become universalized in our culture and has therefore become a kind of lens through which we interpret a character's life and development. According to Lloyd Baugh,

> The Christ-figure is neither Jesus nor the Christ, but rather a shadow, a faint glimmer or reflection of him. As a fully human being, the Christ figure may be weak, uncertain, even a sinner, that is may have all the limits of any human being in the situation at hand. The Christ-figure is a foil to Jesus Christ, and between the two figures there is a reciprocal relationship. On the one hand, the reference to Christ clarifies the situation of the Christ-figure and adds depth to the significance of his actions; on the other hand, the person and situation of the Christ-figure can provide new understanding of who and how Christ is.[5]

Though we will have an opportunity to examine a trio of Jesus films in the next chapter and several films featuring Christ-figures in subsequent chapters, in this chapter we explore a film that is a unique interweaving of both. *Jesus of Montreal* (1989), directed by Denys Arcand, tells the story of a young actor named Daniel Coulombe (played by Lothaire Bluteau) who has been given the assignment of updating a nearly defunct and poorly attended open-air passion play at a local Catholic shrine in Montreal. The film traces Daniel's efforts to research who Jesus was in historical context and then to assemble a theater troupe to create and perform a play about Jesus. As Daniel goes about "calling" four other actors to join him and through repeated performances of the play, his life becomes an allegory of Christ's, and he even begins actually to take on characteristics of Christ.

Because Daniel's version of the passion play is so unorthodox, the church orders an end to the performances. In defiance, the actors insist on performing the play a last time. As Daniel is hanging on the cross in one of the last stations of the play, security guards interrupt, a scuffle ensues, and somehow the cross is toppled, crushing Daniel and knocking him out. Daniel briefly regains consciousness and, though dazed, wanders the subways, preaching lines from the gospels to waiting passengers (an allusion to Christ's descent into hell). Daniel finally expires, and his body is rushed to the hospital and placed on an operating table with arms outstretched in the shape of a cross. In an attempt to construct an allegory of the resurrection, the film culminates with

Jesus of Montreal
© Max Films International, Courtesy MoMA

Daniel's heart and eyes being transplanted through organ donation and with the creation of a theater company in his memory.

Throughout the film, Arcand, who is known for his cynical and biting criticism of Western civilization,[6] pits Daniel against the materialism and consumerism of Québec society. In a scene reminiscent of Christ's cleansing of the temple, Daniel intervenes in the case of one of his fellow actors, Mireille, who is being sexually exploited during auditions for a beer commercial. The religious overtones to the beer jingle reinforce Arcand's indictment of the idolatrous nature of the advertising industry ("The young crowd's here, we worship beer,""Nothing's sacred to you but a good glass of brew"). When Mireille is ordered to bare her breasts on stage or lose the job, Daniel charges forward, turns over tables, destroys video equipment, strikes the director, and chases others away with a whip made of electrical cords. In another case, a handsome, smooth-talking lawyer named Richard Cardinal (a word play on the powerful Cardinal Richilieu of fourteenth-century France) takes Daniel to the top of a skyscraper and, like the devil he is meant to symbolize, tempts Daniel with fame and fortune if he will cooperate with the lawyer's plans to market and commercialize Daniel's career. As they look out over Montreal, Cardinal whispers furtively to Daniel,"with your talent, this city is yours if you want it."

Arcand (who shows up briefly on screen as a judge) also finds several ways to set his Christ-figure over against the corruption and irrelevance of the institutional church. In the passion play scene where Jesus is supposed to confront the wealth and hypocrisy of the Jewish religious establishment, Daniel recites his lines while gazing directly at the church leaders who have shown up to watch the play. And when Father Leclerc cancels the play, Daniel rebukes him for his cowardice and inconsistency. Leclerc, the priest who solicited Daniel's help in the first place, is worried that the play will offend traditional sensibilities and contradict the official teachings of the church. Ultimately, he is worried about his own job security. As Leclerc admits, "Institutions live longer than individuals." The insecure priest has always taken the safe route in life, and his useless-ness corresponds to the uselessness of a church that is little more than a narcotic for, as he says, a "gathering of universal misery." In *Jesus of Montreal*, the true Christ-figure is forced to stand up against the very church that has come after him and claims to represent him.[7]

Daniel also provides a metaphor for Christ in his interactions with the group of actors he has assembled, especially the women. Just as he calls them from their various walks of life (in the case of one actor, Constance, he utters only the words,"I've come for you"), so he lives, eats, and builds community with them. They are not followers in the sense of robots or mindless sheep; they clearly re-tain their own subjectivity. They are participants in shaping the script, even to the extent that one of the actors is allowed to include Hamlet's soliloquy simply because he had always wanted to perform it! Nonetheless, it is clearly Daniel who is the glue and visionary leader of the group—the one who most centrally internalizes the significance of the play and embodies the communal mission of the actors.

The most transparent parallels to the life of Christ are, of course, contained in the final film sequences involving Daniel's persecution, death on a cross, and resurrection. Other parallels, however, include a John the Baptist character in the form of a young actor who shows up in the first scenes of the film. While being congratulated by his fans after one of his performances, the actor sees Daniel, points to him, and says, "*There* is a good actor!" An advertising executive who sees this young actor "wants his head" for one of her ad campaigns and, like the story of John the Baptist and Salome, she is apparently successful, for in the closing scenes of the film, Daniel spots the young actor's head on a billboard posted in the subway station and becomes sickened by it.

In another scene, Daniel is washed by Mireille, creating a correspondence to Mary Magdalene, who washed Jesus after she had been rescued from a life of prostitution. In Mireille's case, the prostitution has come in the service of the advertising industry and a series of exploitative relationships with men who have seen her as little more than a sexual object. As the group of actors eat pizza together before their final performance (a "Last Supper" of sorts), she encourages them not to give up. "You saved me," she confesses.

The film is never less than obvious in establishing parallels between Daniel and Jesus ("He's got a type of blood that's a Godsend!" says the organ transplant doctor), and yet what is unique about *Jesus of Montreal* is the way Arcand intersperses a number of other portraits of Jesus in creative tension with the Christ-figure that is developing in Daniel's character. Centrally, of course, there is the passion play itself. It is an intense and eclectic hodgepodge of gospel text and commentary that attempts to present the life and death of Jesus in the context of the ancient Near East. In preparing the script, Daniel has done his own research into the Jesus of historical scholarship, and the end product is a passion play that comes off as more realistic, gritty, and down-to-earth than the overly reverent and highly stylized version that had previously been performed. At the same time, the play is scandalous because, for example, it calls into question the virgin birth by suggesting that Jesus was the illegitimate son of a Roman soldier and presents Jesus not as a miracle-worker, but as a magician who grew up in Egypt, "the cradle of magic."

None of these radically different candidates for portraying Jesus is ultimately satisfying in the film—the demythologized Jesus of historical scholarship, the lofty Jesus of tradition, the amalgamation that Daniel puts together, even the large sculpture of Christ that stands in the middle of the shrine itself. But these portraits are not finally what Arcand is selling us. They are, as Baugh notes, "foils or contrasting background to the Christ-figuring of Daniel. Arcand couches his social-moral-cultural criticism of Québec society precisely in the contrast, the dynamic confrontation between Daniel as Christ-figure and the Jesus-portraits among which he moves."[8]

At one point in the film, for example, Daniel is in a library conducting research for the play when he encounters a librarian who asks him if he is looking for Jesus. When Daniel answers, "Yes," the librarian responds in words that will turn out to be central to the entire film: "It's he who will find you." Arcand is here, as throughout the film, relativizing the various portraits of Jesus—whether they are popular or scholarly, conservative or liberal, secular or religious. In this and countless other ways, *Jesus of Montreal* keeps the question burning before us, "Who is Jesus, really?"

The Christ of the Creed

It is impossible to read the second section of the Apostles' Creed and miss the fact that the bulk of it is devoted to narrating key events in Jesus' life. Early on in the creed's development, two originally different types of creedal statements were most likely linked together: the three-part baptismal confession (with its three "I believe" declarations) and a short account of the "Jesus story" derived largely from the gospels. Apparently, the earliest Christians believed that including this brief historical narrative provided important clues about what it might mean to exercise faith in Jesus and thereby live in a way that is loyal to him. Just as Daniel grasps who Jesus is (and is himself grasped by Jesus) through the telling and retelling of the passion play, so also the creed confesses the identity of Jesus through its narration of Jesus' conception, birth, suffering, crucifixion, death, burial, resurrection, ascension, and coming judgment.

These events are not merely pieces of historical trivia thrown in to fill space. They are loaded with theological meaning. Upon close inspection, however, we find that the creed does not begin this section with a narrative of Jesus' life, but with three bold assertions about who Jesus is: "Christ," "God's only son," and "our Lord." Each of these three titles represents a distinct approach to Jesus, and together they form a framework for interpreting the key events in his life. In the remainder of this chapter we will examine these three titles in conversation with *Jesus of Montreal* in order to determine what they suggest to us about the significance of Jesus.

Jesus, "the Christ"—the Approach from Before

It may go without saying, but *Christ* is not Jesus' last name! And though, over the last two thousand years, the two words have almost come to function together as his proper name (a practice that can be traced as far back as the apostle Paul), to say "Jesus Christ" is already to make a faith affirmation. To say "Jesus Christ" is to affirm that Jesus[9] is the *Christ*—the *anointed one*, the *Messiah* of the Jews. Those three tiny words ("of the Jews") are important. The word *Christ* has a uniquely historical context in Judaism and cannot adequately be understood apart from the history of the Jewish people. That is not to say that Jesus cannot be spoken of as the *Christ* today in a non-Jewish context, but if we wish to understand the meaning of this title in *any* context, it is in Judaism that we must find our starting point. To speak of Jesus as the *Christ*, therefore, is to approach his significance "from before"—from the perspective of a long history of hope and expectation that one day the liberator of God would appear on earth to usher in a new order—the "reign of God."

The function of the Christ in Jewish expectation is both positive and negative. Positively, the Christ would be a king who would establish *shalom*: a unity of peace and justice that not only transforms interpersonal relationships, but achieves the welfare of the entire social, political, and economic order, including even human relations with the wider ecosystem of plants and animals. The coming

Christ would be a champion of the poor and defender of the widowed and the fatherless. Hope in the Christ was, for the Jewish people, a hope that God had concrete plans for them as a people and that such a person would be anointed by God to inaugurate these plans in terms of a holistic and integrated condition of personal and communal well-being—a model for all the nations.

Negatively, the Christ was also the one who would eliminate all obstacles to *shalom* and throw off the chains of oppression, war, and injustice. The messiah would cast down the wicked and proud from their positions of arrogance, calling an end to their exploitative practices. There is an inescapably subversive dimension to authentic messianic hope. *Shalom* does not appear without a great reversal and shaking up of the status quo. What the Jewish people understood was that the forces of oppression that keep people impoverished and alienated from each other and from creation have much to lose with the advent of the *anointed one*. With justice comes judgment, and the coming of the Christ requires nothing short of a revolution as God's enemies are defeated and the apparatus of their domination is exposed and dismantled.

It is hard to know precisely what the disciples may have had in mind when, as in the case of Peter, they first confessed Jesus to be the Christ (Mt. 16:16). We do know that on many occasions, Jesus was reluctant to use the title himself. The term certainly carried political connotations of a restored kingdom like that of David. And although Jesus may not have fulfilled crass expectations of a reestablished monarchy or, as in the case of the Zealots, an overthrow of Roman domination, he certainly engaged in political confrontation (see chapter 6). In confessing Jesus to be the *Christ*, the disciples saw in him the possibility of a new way of living that was very much "here and now" with concrete political, economic, spiritual, and social dimensions. So also today when we confess Jesus as the *Christ*, we confess his relevance for every aspect of our lives and not merely the private and interior aspects related to personal morality and devotion.[10]

Do the messianic dimensions of Christ come through in the film *Jesus of Montreal?* There are two prominent ways in which they might. There is, of course, the Jesus of the passion play. This Jesus is simple and down-to-earth, a far cry from the reverential treatment of Jesus in the older Hollywood spectacles. The passion play in *Jesus of Montreal* clearly asserts the Jewishness of Jesus, but the concrete social, political, and religious dimensions of that Jewishness are largely undeveloped,[11] and so it is difficult for the play to portray Jesus as an individual who either fulfills or contradicts Jewish messianic expectations.

Through the use of Daniel as Christ-figure, however, the film virtually explodes with the messianic dimensions of Jesus' ministry—especially in its more negative and antagonistic aspects. In order to accomplish this, the film must translate the Jesus of ancient Israel into twentieth-century Québec, which it does precisely through Daniel's confrontation with the advertising industry, on the one hand, and the institutional church, on the other. In fact, through the use of a nonliteral Christ-figure, *Jesus of Montreal* is able to convey to us the sociopolitical and economic dimensions of what it means to be the *Christ* of the Jews more powerfully, perhaps, than a straightforward historical portrayal of Jesus in his native Jewish context could. It is helpful to understand historically how Jesus' announcement of the reign of God challenged the oppressive grip of political, economic, and religious systems in Judea and why Jesus would have been perceived by so many of his time as dangerous and subversive. A strong "Jesus film" or passion play might be able to do this well (though few, in fact, do). But if we wish our affirmation of Jesus as the *Christ* to be more than merely a claim about what happened in the past, that affirmation must be contextualized in terms of the forces that oppress and hinder personal and social well-being today, such as an insidious materialism or the blind consumerism that feeds on that materialism. To confess Jesus as the Christ in our time is to allow his announcement of God's reign to be heard clearly in the context of our own contemporary idolatries and enslavements.

When it comes to Daniel's confrontation of the institutional church in *Jesus of Montreal*, this contextualization of Jesus as the Christ is especially powerful. One of the unfortunate side effects of standard portrayals of Jesus' messianic identity in many Jesus films (and in a considerable amount of Christian preaching over the years) is their implicit and explicit anti-Semitism. Jewish religious leaders—the priests, scribes, lawyers, and Pharisees—are the culprits for failing to recognize the Christ and even blocking the very *shalom* that the Christ comes to institute. But this historical "scapegoating" can easily distract Christians from perceiving our own unwillingness to accept the Christ and to recognize where he is at work today. Arcand beautifully intersects the passion play's portrayal of Jesus as he confronts Jewish religious officials with Daniel as he confronts officials of the institutional church. The film thereby contextualizes Jesus' messianic role as prophet and critic of all religious systems that claim to be bearers of God's reign, but instead function practically as an obstacle to it. In fact, in *Jesus of Montreal*, the anti-Semitism of traditional Christianity is even reversed. When Daniel is first injured he is taken to the emergency room of St. Mark's hospital (obviously a Christian hospital), where he is neglected and ignored. The hospital staff does not have time for him, and his friends are instructed to take a number and wait in line. When he collapses a second time, he is taken to a Jewish hospital, where he is given immediate and careful attention and his friends are received warmly by the hospital staff. The contrast is obvious. As Arcand hints throughout the film, Christians today may not be all that different from the Pharisees of Jesus' day, and it is possible that Christ is being crucified all over again—this time by the church.

If *Jesus of Montreal* suffers in its portrayal of the messianic dimensions of Jesus' ministry, it is to the extent that it focuses almost exclusively on the more negative and critical side of what it means to be the Christ—exposing and denouncing the idolatry of mass advertising, the oppression of consumerism, and the hypocrisy of religion. For a broader understanding of the Christ, what is also needed is a positive announcement or embodiment of what it means to live in *shalom*—the kind of forgiveness, for example, that is depicted in *Dead Man Walking*, or the solidarity and community portrayed in *The Mission* or *Babette's Feast* (these films will be examined in later chapters). *Jesus of Montreal* points dimly toward something more positive in its dramatization of the relationships between Daniel and the other actors, but we catch only vague glimpses of the *shalom* toward which they might be moving.

Jesus, "God's Only Son"—the Approach from Above

In Matthew's gospel, when Peter confesses that Jesus is the Christ, he also adds the words "the Son of the living God." In the ancient world, the title "son of God" was used of kings, priests, or other persons who were recognized to have a divine calling or election.

In the Old Testament, Israel is spoken of metaphorically as God's son (Ex. 4:22; Hos. 11:1). With Christ, however, something much more profound is being affirmed. To speak of Jesus as "God's only son" is to claim a unique relationship between Jesus and God—one of utter transparency to who God is and what God wants. The gospel of John puts it this way: Jesus is the decisive embodiment of God's "will" or "purpose" (*logos* in Greek).[12] Thus, the title "Son of God" is a way of approaching the significance of Jesus, figuratively speaking, "from above." Rather than starting with Jewish expectation and moving toward Jesus as the *Christ* "from before," this approach starts with God's character and purpose and then moves toward understanding how that character and purpose are *incarnate* in Jesus as the Son of God.

To say that we are approaching Jesus "from above" can be misleading, however. It is not as if the disciples already knew God and then happened to recognize God's presence in Jesus. Rather, these first Christians claimed that it was in Jesus that they came to know God. In the Apostles' Creed, we are affirming that Jesus is utterly transparent to and dependent on God ("The Son can do nothing of his own accord, but only what he sees the Father doing" Jn. 5:19 RSV), but we are also affirming that we really don't know God adequately until we look at Jesus.

In the New Testament, Jesus is the "firstborn" Son of God,[13] not for mere status, but for the distinct purpose, as our elder brother, of calling us into the family of God. To affirm that Jesus is God's Son, therefore, is to open ourselves up to the possibility of also becoming God's sons and daughters. We, of course, do not bear the same transparency to God as Jesus does. And yet it is precisely the kind of openness to God's grace and holiness found in Jesus to which we also are called.

Jesus of Montreal does not attempt to portray the relationship between Jesus and God in any explicit way. Whether this happens on a figurative level, however, is open to interpretation, especially given the fact that director Arcand is a nonbeliever who is nonetheless interested in asking about Jesus' significance for us today. There is, however, something rather miraculous about Daniel's transformation into a Christ-figure that suggests a power beyond himself that has graciously transformed him and that does not appear to have been contrived on his own or produced through his own hard work. Early on in the film we know he is seeking "inspiration." One could make the argument that as Daniel the actor increasingly recedes into the background through the course of the film and his role as Christ-figure comes increasingly into focus, he is becoming God's incarnation.

And yet it is also possible to conclude that the film implicitly rejects the notion of Jesus as God's Son by discarding the virgin birth, for example, or by interpreting Jesus' healing ministry as the performance of magic. As we have seen, however, it is difficult to place too much emphasis on the Jesus portrayed in Daniel's passion play; that is not really the image of Jesus that Arcand is trying to communicate to us. It more often serves as a foil for the more important Christ-figure developing in Daniel. Still, it is clear that Arcand has accentuated the elements in Jesus' life and teaching that translate well into contemporary social criticism and that do not necessarily require that there even be a God or that Jesus be the Son of God. Daniel symbolizes Jesus' role as a great ethical teacher, liberator, and prophet. There is, however, little sense of a wider horizon or transcendence against which the Christ-figure's life, death, and resurrection can be placed that would point us toward God. Like Monty Python's Brian, Daniel more or less stumbles into his messianic role. It may be that in *Jesus of Montreal* Arcand is not so much denying that Jesus is the Son of God as he is merely sidestepping the question. But without providing some way on film of giving Daniel's character a transcendent dimension, Daniel cannot be transparent (for what would he be transparent to?) and, instead, comes off as simply fanatical or odd.

Jesus, *"Our Lord"*—*the Approach from Below*

One of the earliest Christian confessions known to us is the simple phrase "Jesus is Lord"—a phrase loaded with religious and political significance. Not only was *Lord* a title used in emperor worship and in other religions and cults of the ancient Near East, it was also the term used by Jews to translate the name of God in the Greek version of the scriptures. The word once used for God was now being used for Jesus as a way of pledging loyalty to him in explicit contrast to other competing loyalties in the world! We might say that attributing to Jesus the title "our Lord," therefore, is a way of approaching the significance of Jesus "from below"—from the standpoint of our obedience and discipleship, from the standpoint of our deepest allegiances and the pattern of life that we intend to follow. To call Jesus "our Lord" undoubtedly says something about his identity or divine origin, but it is ultimately a way of saying something about the way we intend to lead our lives.

Bringing forward the word *Lord* into our own twenty-first-century context, however, is fraught with difficulties. In the New Testament, the word *lord* could literally mean "owner" or "master," and in feudal societies such as those in which Christianity has been immersed for much of its existence, some rather oppressive connotations came to attach themselves to this word. We don't use the word very much in normal conversation today because we don't live in a time where we as individuals, families, or groups are placed as *vassals* under the dominion of another person such as was the case in the Middle Ages. And when we do use the word *lord* we often do so in a negative way to indicate domination and arrogance ("don't lord yourself over me!"). So, for example, when Darth Vader is referred to as "Lord Vader" in *Star Wars*, audiences acquire a heightened sense of his power and control. But is this really the way we want to talk about Jesus, or is there too much excess baggage associated with the term? Might we end up saying the very opposite of what we mean to say by continuing to call Jesus *Lord*?

It may be helpful to know that Jesus himself was not content to allow this term to be applied to him without first transforming its meaning—and this he did by coupling it with servanthood. Jesus explicitly talks about his lordship in the context of washing the disciples' feet:

> And so when He had washed their feet, and taken His garments, and reclined at the table again, He said to them, "Do you know what I have done to you? You call Me Teacher and Lord; and you are right, for so I am. If I then, the Lord and the Teacher, washed your feet, you also ought to wash one another's feet. For I gave you an example that you also should do as I did to you." (Jn. 13:12–15)

To call Jesus *Lord* is to take upon ourselves Jesus' own brand of power—namely, the power of unconditional, self-giving love that includes placing ourselves in the service of others. To call Jesus *Lord* is to renounce control, selfishness, and the destructive attempt to dominate and manipulate others. As Theodore Jennings says, "The ascription of lordship to Jesus is authentic only insofar as it entails the abolition of all structures of lordship within the community of Jesus. For only so is it possible to emulate the one who has chosen to be servant of all."[14]

To call someone "my teacher" reveals that I consider myself "his student." To call someone "my boss" means I think of myself as "her employee." To call two people "my parents" is just another way of saying I am "their son." So what are we saying when we call Jesus *Lord*? What is implied about who we are? Are we Jesus' slaves? vassals? property? If it is true that Jesus comes to bring an end to all systems of domination and subordination and to the treatment of human beings as objects and property, then none of these correlates is adequate. According to the New Testament, to say "Jesus is Lord" is to affirm that I am his *disciple*. It is *discipleship* that is the correlate to Jesus' *lordship*. To call Jesus *Lord* is to affirm our loyalty to him by following him, imitating him, learning from him, and, indeed, loving him. In fact, Jesus delivers a serious warning about even calling him "Lord" if we are not going to engage in discipleship:

> Not everyone who says to Me, "Lord, Lord," will enter the kingdom of heaven; but he who does the will of My Father who is in heaven. Many will say to Me on that day, "Lord, Lord, did we not prophesy in Your name, and in Your name cast out demons, and in Your name perform many miracles?" And then I will declare to them, "I never knew you; depart from me, you who practice lawlessness." (Mt. 7:21–23)

We have already noted how *Jesus of Montreal* sets up an important contrast between the Christ-figure of Daniel and a number of other competing portraits of Jesus, not least of which is the passion play itself. It is in and through this contrast that one of the central themes of the film is developed—namely, the difference between merely giving lip service to Jesus, or even recognizing his importance as a historical figure, and actually *following* Jesus. So, for example, theater critics and fans simply fall in love with Daniel's portrayal of Jesus, and yet there is no indication that they have grasped what it really means to confess Jesus as Lord. In one case, an admirer talking to the actors after the play feigns a real appreciation for the Jesus they have just portrayed: "Jesus is so gentle; He's so…positive."

It is clear, however, that he hasn't a clue what he's talking about, since he also believes that astronauts have discovered that the moon is hollow but "can't let on."

So also, the lawyer, Richard Cardinal, loves the Jesus of the passion play primarily because he sees a way to cash in on Jesus. After all, as he says, "Jesus has become fashionable these days." This vulgar commercialization of Jesus climaxes in the memorial theater company instigated by Cardinal after Daniel's death. The memorial is an obvious symbol representing the church and thereby reinforcing the film's indictment of the church as fundamentally anti-Christ, a commercial exploitation of the true Christ's memory. In one of the most profound ironies of the film, Christ is resurrected through his donated organs, a bodily way of portraying resurrection. The church, however, which the New Testament calls the "body of Christ" (Eph. 4:12), is not depicted as the body of Christ at all, but rather as a distortion and corruption of who Christ is. Indeed, it is depicted as an institution dreamed up by the devil himself (if we are consistent with the treatment of Cardinal as the devil elsewhere in the film).

The world portrayed in *Jesus of Montreal* is bathed in Jesus-images, and yet the lordship of Jesus rarely penetrates that world and the lives of the people who live in it. Sadly, according to the film, the church may be the most unwilling to follow Jesus as Lord. Symbolized by Father Leclerc, the church is too often more concerned with maintaining its orthodoxy and institutional structures than with actually following Christ's way. To follow Christ as Lord is costly. It requires a radical shift in our priorities and values. That is why, throughout the New Testament, discipleship always begins with repentance and conversion. It is only as we set aside the terrible burden of always having to be lord (or of allowing other persons and forces in our lives to serve as lord) that Jesus himself can finally become Lord—Lord of our lives and Lord of the church.

QUESTIONS FOR DISCUSSION

1. In what ways does the life of Daniel parallel or symbolize the life of Christ? Are there other characters in the film who function metaphorically as characters in Christ's life?
2. There may be as many different views about who Jesus was as there are people who think about Jesus. What different versions or representations of Jesus do you detect in this film?

3. What do you think the director is trying to convey in this film? Is there a message you think the film is attempting to send?

4. What does it mean to call Jesus the "Christ"? the "Son of God"? "our Lord"?

RELATED FILMS

Braveheart (1995)
Cool Hand Luke (1967)
Monty Python's Life of Brian (1979)
The Matrix (1999)

NOTES

[1] The word *passion* is used to describe Jesus' final experience of suffering leading up to his crucifixion.

[2] Lloyd Baugh, *Imaging the Divine: Jesus and Christ-Figures in Film* (Kansas City: Sheed & Ward, 1997), 9.

[3] Peter T. Chattaway, "Jesus in the Movies," *Bible Review* (February 1998): 28.

[4] For more on the distinction between a "Christ film" and a "Jesus film," see Baugh.

[5] Ibid., 112.

[6] See, for example, Arcand's film *The Decline of the American Empire* (1985).

[7] *Monty Python's Life of Brian* (1979) can be read as conveying very much the same message. Given the title, the film may appear to be a satire of the life of Christ. The satire, however, is almost always directed toward the followers of Christ, who are more preoccupied with infighting and with creating institutional structures to ensure self-perpetuation.

[8] Baugh, 115.

[9] The name "Jesus" itself is the Greek form of the Jewish name "Joshua" or "Yeshua," which, though it literally means "Salvation is in Yahweh," was a common name among Jewish males of the time.

[10] Unfortunately, it has now become commonplace among Christians to claim that what the Jews looked for was a political kingdom and what Christ brought was instead a spiritual one. While it is certainly true that Jesus' politics were not politics as usual, this view misses the full implications of what it means to claim Jesus as the *Christ* and creates a false dualism where for Jesus there is only one all-inclusive reality—the reign of God.

[11] For an interesting study in this regard, see Adele Reinhartz, "Jesus in Film: Hollywood Perspectives on the Jewishness of Jesus," *Journal of Religion and Film* 2, no. 2 (Fall 1998).

[12] John 1:1, 14.

[13] Romans 8:29; Colossians 1:15; Revelation 3:14.

[14] Jennings, *Loyalty to God*, 83.

5

"Conceived by the Holy Spirit and born of the Virgin Mary"

 **A Trio of Jesus Films:**
The Greatest Story Ever Told,
The Last Temptation of Christ, **and**
The Gospel According to
St. Matthew

One of the most perplexing questions in the Christian faith is how we are to understand the relationship between God's gracious and sovereign activity and human response in freedom and obedience. The single reference to the birth of Jesus in the Apostles' Creed is a prime example of this relationship. The creed affirms that Jesus had his origins in the activity and initiative of God the Holy Spirit, and yet it also states that Jesus was born of a woman named Mary and therefore shares with the rest of us the full human condition. On the one hand, to say that Jesus was conceived of the Holy Spirit and born of a virgin is to affirm that we have been saved by grace[1] and that, as humans, we are utterly incapable of producing a savior on our own. Jesus is God's gift and initiative. On the other hand, however, we are not saying that Jesus had a "jazzed-up" genetic code or superhuman ability. In the early centuries of Christianity, some believers were so intent on asserting the deity of Jesus that they ended up denying his earthly, bodily, and human origins.[2] For them, the creed's affirmation that Jesus was born of Mary was downright offensive. In fact, the word *born* would have been more scandalous to them than the word *virgin*.[3] Given the fact that many Christians today understand the virgin birth as an assertion of Jesus' divinity, it is important to remember that among the early Christians the virgin birth was a deliberate way of emphasizing his full humanity.

How we understand the paradox of Jesus' double origins is only the tip of an iceberg that in virtually every area of Christian experience includes how we construe the relationship between the divine and the human. This tension shows up, for example, in how we understand salvation as the product of divine grace and, at the same time, human faith. It surfaces in our regard for the Bible as divinely inspired and, at the same time, a document written by ordinary, fallible humans. It crops up yet again in how we are able to think of the church as an imperfect human institution and, at the same time, a creation of the Holy Spirit. In fact, Mary's prominent role in the Apostles' Creed is a testimony to her own embodiment of this tension. God chooses Mary, and it is by the power of the Holy Spirit that she conceives a child. Mary, however, is not merely an object of God's grace or an empty receptacle into which God deposits a gift. Mary is a willing and obedient servant who has "found favor with God" and who consents to Gods' activity in her life ("be it done to me according to your word"). It is both because of her divine election and because of her obedience and trust that Christians of all generations consider Mary "blessed" and aspire to imitate her faith.

If Christians across the centuries have consistently struggled to hold in tension the full humanity and full divinity of Jesus without letting one of these overshadow or negate the other, perhaps we can begin to appreciate how difficult it is to maintain this paradox on film. A perennial problem in films about Jesus is how to present him as a real human being and, at the same time, as the one Christians believe to be Messiah, Son of God, and Lord. Consider, for example, the difficulty of providing a sense of historical authenticity in the film while at the same time giving due consideration to the fact that the gospels are evangelistic accounts written, as John says, "that you may believe that Jesus is the Christ, the Son of God" (20:31). The problem here is not that the gospel accounts are inaccurate or untrustworthy, but that they are written with a particular agenda and an unavoidable partiality that does not provide us all of the historical, geographical, or chronological details we might like. This, of course, leaves the writer of a screenplay in an unenviable position. Should Jesus say only what is in the gospel texts, or is it permissible to write additional dialogue for the Son of God that would help us to see him in normal human interactions—at break-fast, work, weddings, walking down the road, or fishing?

Add to these difficulties the fact that in constructing a screen-play, Jesus films have four gospels to choose from, each of them with its own unique perspective and approach. Should a Jesus film attempt to harmonize all four gospels into one story or instead be more selective, relying perhaps on only one? Early on in the forma-tion of the New Testament, Christians decided that it was impor-tant to include all four gospels side-by-side without attempting to harmonize them into one single gospel. A film, however, must make a choice.

On top of all this is the perplexing question of how to signal Jesus' humanity and divinity on film. Go too far in one direction and the film will be viewed as disrespectful and blasphemous; go too far in the other direction and Jesus becomes a mythical figure, far removed from our own concrete life situations. In this chapter we will look briefly at three Jesus films to see how they fare in pulling off this incredibly difficult synthesis between reverence and relevance. Whether or not any or all of these three films finally prove satisfactory in this regard, perhaps they can nonetheless illus-trate for us some of the issues at stake in our affirmation that Jesus of Nazareth is both the purpose of God incarnate and the truly human one.

The Greatest Story Ever Told (1965)

The 1950s were full of large-scale biblical epics such as *David and Bathsheba* (1951), *The Robe* (1953), *The Ten Commandments* (1956), *Ben Hur* (1959), and *Spartacus* (1960). Perhaps it was inevitable, there-fore, that the Jesus story would be pressed into this mold, which eventually it was in the form of *King of Kings* (1961) and *The Greatest Story Ever Told* (1965). Both films featured elaborate and expensive sets, wide-screen formats with brilliant colors, pounding musical scores, and a cast of thousands, including loads of famous actors. In addition, both films seem to drag on interminably.

In *The Greatest Story Ever Told*, director George Stevens attempted to provide natural landscapes similar to that of Palestine by filming in the deserts of southern Utah and Colorado. The strategy back-fired, however, as moviegoers were apparently all too familiar with the canyons, cliffs, mountains, and rivers of the great American South-west. They were instead distracted by the inappropriateness of an ancient Jerusalem rising up among the sharp bluffs and ravines of the Wild West, John's baptisms accommodated by the churning Colo-rado River, and the Sea of Galilee set against the backdrop of the majestic, snowcapped Rocky Mountains!

What is most striking about *The Greatest Story Ever Told*, how-ever, is how strongly it attempts to assert the deity of Christ with barely a hint of his humanity or Jewish origins—a strategy that finally works against itself by turning Jesus into an impersonal icon or religious postcard. The film is framed at the beginning and end with a fresco of Jesus on a church wall—similar to Byzantine images of the *Christos Pantocrator*, a kind of cosmic lord who is suspended over the earth in the clouds. To reinforce this reverent portrait of an otherworldly Jesus, the narrator is at the same time reading from the prologue of John, the gospel that most strongly asserts the deity of Christ: "In the beginning was the word, and the word was with God, and the word was God." The face of Jesus in the painting is that of Max von Sydow, the Swedish actor (at that time relatively unknown in America) cast by Stevens to play the part of Jesus.

Throughout the film, Von Sydow's Jesus speaks with a distinctly European accent and with the archaic tone and refined vocabulary of the King James Bible, in sharp contrast to virtually everyone around him who speaks in common English vernacular. [4] This dis-traction is never more ridiculous than after Jesus' final words on the cross, "Father, into thy hands I commit my Spirit." These words, spoken slowly and melodramatically on quavering lips, are imme-diately followed by pouring rain, violins, choirs, and then, from out of nowhere, John Wayne's only appearance in the film as the centu-rion who sluggishly drawls, "Truly, this man was the Son o' Gawd."

Von Sydow's Jesus is overly dramatic, habitually pausing in mid-sentence to strike a pose (even when clearing out the temple), ex-tending his arms and hands with wide motions as he speaks, and regularly casting his eyes toward the heavens. The lines that this

Jesus speaks are as otherworldly as his demeanor. The film frequently has Jesus talk about why he has "come into this world" and has him repeatedly say that his kingdom is "not of this world." It is therefore easy to agree with Fred Myers, film reviewer for the *Christian Century*, who in 1965 wrote, "This Jesus Christ sounds like a creature from a different universe."[5] The strategy of presenting Jesus in his ethereal, cosmic dimensions continues throughout the entire film until its conclusion when, against the backdrop of "The Hallelujah Chorus," Jesus, "risen and swollen to cyclopean proportions,"[6] ascends into the clouds. Never mind that "The Hallelujah Chorus" has already been used at the raising of Lazarus to march us triumphantly into the intermission. Stevens pushes whatever buttons need to be pushed and as often as necessary in order to inflate the hearts of his viewers with reverence and devotion for Christ.

The Greatest Story Ever Told demonstrates how inadequate, tiresome, and silly Hollywood clichés can be when attempting to signal religious faith and devotion or the presence of the divine. These are notoriously difficult to depict through dialogue alone, so Stevens adds trumpets, violins, and choirs of angels with perhaps a pained expression or two to depict intense piety. Another device is lighting, which Stevens exploits as far as is cinematically possible. Stevens has Jesus be tempted by the devil for a solid five minutes against the backdrop of a huge green moon at one point in the film. Elsewhere, sunsets and sunrises are employed strategically as well as orange and blue-purple filters at the resurrection. At the Last Supper, Jesus and his disciples line up along one side of the table, in imitation of Leonardo daVinci's fresco, facing the camera instead of each other. Jesus stands under the precise center of an archway in the scene and is backlit, producing a halo effect. Likewise, when Jesus prays in the garden of Gethsemane, we get the same left profile as the famous Greco-Sallman portrait with backlighting.

One of the strangest scenes in the film is when Jesus holds a torchlight rally in the temple square. As he addresses the throngs late into the evening, looking a bit like the Statue of Liberty, he quotes, oddly enough, from Saint Paul, who has yet to write the lines, "faith, hope and love abide...these three, but the greatest of these is love." In the end, however, the license the screenplay takes with the story of Jesus[7] is not nearly as disturbing as the extreme otherworldliness of this Jesus. The film goes overboard in portraying Jesus from the very beginning as the Word of God incarnate and as the one who understands himself clearly as the Messiah and who is not afraid to say so. Long gone is the messianic secret in Matthew, Mark, or Luke, with the frequent injunction by Jesus to "tell no one." Instead, under the heavy influence of John's gospel, *The Greatest Story Ever Told* has Jesus seize any and every opportunity to proclaim himself the "salvation of the world."[8]

Though Satan plays a severely restricted role in the four gospels, he pops up everywhere throughout *The Greatest Story Ever Told*—among the crowds, in the temple courtyard, and even bumping into Judas on his way to betray Jesus. The strategy here is again to demonstrate that Jesus is not of this world and that his real opposition is not political, human, or religious, but otherworldly. Thus, it is not the Jews or the Romans who are responsible for crucifying Jesus in this film; it is Satan himself who shows up in the crowd and starts the chant, "Crucify him!"

More than likely, this overly divinized portrait of Jesus was the end result of Stevens' attempt at accomplishing his goal of universalizing Christ's message of compassion for people of all faiths.[9] As Stevens once put it, "The basic theme of the story…relates to the universality of [people] and how they must learn to live together."[10] Stevens apparently believed that by removing Jesus from his earthly, sociopolitical, and human context, his message could be made more accessible to more people. But this misses precisely the scandal of the gospel—that in a specific time, place, and context God's purpose for humankind has been revealed in the son of a Jewish carpenter. As Lloyd Baugh says,

> What Stevens does not seem to understand is that in a medium as concrete, material and specific as cinema, universalizing Jesus in order to make him the Christ of faith reduces his humanity. In not "dealing with the historical moment" and the cultural reality of Jesus, Stevens loses his human, incarnational dimension, his human nature…The Christ of faith thus becomes a Jesus of myth.[11]

To remove Jesus from his context does not make him relevant for more of the world, but finally makes him irrelevant for all of the world.

The Last Temptation of Christ (1988)

If *The Greatest Story Ever Told* distances Jesus from his human origins and social context, thereby hoping reverently to universalize his message, *The Last Temptation of Christ* also hopes to make Jesus more universally accessible, but by provocation rather than reverence. It attempts to strip away the conventional Hollywood trappings of previous Jesus films and instead to concentrate on the human dimension. Based on the 1955 novel of the same name by Nikos Kazantzakis and directed by Martin Scorsese, *The Last Temptation of Christ* is undoubtedly the most controversial Jesus film in history and one that rushes headlong into the tension between deity and humanity in Jesus. The film's opening credits quote Kazantzakis:

> The dual substance of Christ—the yearning, so human, so superhuman, of man to attain God...has always been a deep inscrutable mystery to me. My principal anguish and source of all my joys and sorrows from my youth onward has been the incessant, merciless battle between the spirit and the flesh...and my soul is the arena where these two armies have clashed and met.

The film then adds the disclaimer, "This film is not based upon the Gospels but upon this fictional exploration of the eternal spiritual conflict."

Despite the disclaimer, *The Last Temptation* is clearly a portrayal of the life of Jesus with most of the standard characters, events, and teachings drawn from the gospels. Filmed in Morocco, the entire film has a dusty, Middle Eastern authenticity about it (though the exotic score and other sound effects are sometimes more Arabic than Jewish[12]). The scandal associated with the film is due primarily to an extended temptation sequence while Jesus is on the cross. Jesus (played by Willem Dafoe) fantasizes that his guardian angel has come to inform him that he is not the Messiah after all and that he can come down from the cross. He is now free to live a normal life as a carpenter and to grow old with a wife and children. Jesus marries Mary Magdalene and, in a scene that was widely objected to, is briefly shown making love to her.[13] After Magdalene dies in childbirth, Jesus weds Mary, the sister of Lazarus, and has several children both by her and her sister, Martha. As the angel says to him,

"There is only one woman in the world; one woman with many faces." Though the larger context here is Jesus' lifelong temptation to abandon self-sacrifice and to embrace instead the normal pleasures of life, love, family, and home, it is the sexual dimension of the temptation that proved to be the most scandalous, especially among conservative Christians.

Insofar as the film suggests that Jesus might have been tempted sexually or with the prospect of an ordinary domestic life, it is on solid theological footing. It would be tragic if Jesus were so elevated in Christian belief that we could not do what *The Last Temptation of Christ* asks us to do, namely, to take with full seriousness the New Testament's claim that Jesus was "tempted in all things as we are, yet without sin" (Heb. 4:15). If this makes Jesus "too human" for us, then it is our christology rather than the film that is flawed. In fact, the film is careful to show that Jesus ultimately does triumph over all these temptations, dying on the cross with the final words, "It is accomplished."

The Last Temptation of Christ
©Universal City Studios, Inc., Courtesy MoMA

The difficulties show up, however, in how the film depicts the temptation sequence, especially when Jesus encounters Paul preaching about the crucified and resurrected Christ despite the fact that Jesus never actually went through with any of it. When Jesus calls Paul a liar, Paul responds, "I created the truth out of what people needed and what they believed. If I have to crucify you to save them, then I'll crucify you. If I have to resurrect you, then I'll do that too." It is not difficult to see how many Christians would perceive inclusion of such a scene as having no purpose other than to insult and offend. Bill Bright, conservative leader of Campus Crusade for Christ, even offered to raise ten million dollars to buy the film in order to destroy it.[14]

As problematic as the temptation sequence might be, what is perhaps more problematic in *The Last Temptation of Christ* is the film's depiction of Jesus prior to this. Scorsese clearly wants to highlight the humanity of Jesus, depicting him as one who "has the doubts we all have" and who "struggles all the time because it's part of his human nature."[15] But the Jesus we see wrestling with a calling from God in *The Last Temptation* is far from normal, and his hangups, doubts, and temptations are nothing at all like those "we all have." More than merely a reluctant Messiah, his having been chosen by God is a source of endless pain, like claws digging beneath his skin. He hears voices and flails around on the dirt clutching at his head. He's not sure if he is possessed by the devil or by God.

In the first scenes of *The Last Temptation,* Jesus is drawn to a message of love and is filled with "pity" for humanity, despite the fact that he more often comes across as a coward and a weakling, especially next to strong characters such as Magdalene and Judas. After his encounter with John the Baptist, however, Jesus turns to preaching radical revolution with an ax in his hand. Jesus then changes his mind again and begins to think of himself as Isaiah's "suffering servant" who must be sacrificed for the sins of the world. This Jesus is not a typical human, who goes through the same stages and struggles that all humans must go through, but an emotional wreck who is engaged in one long identity crisis after another. Scorsese's Jesus is one of the least well-adjusted and most masochistic personalities ever to stumble across the silver screen. Inside him a war is taking place between the flesh and the spirit that is unlike anything most of us might experience. He is full of self-contempt and self-doubt. He whips himself, fasts, and wears a nail-studded belt around his waist. He collaborates with the Romans by making crosses for them so that God will hate him.

For all the protests that the film tarnishes Jesus' divinity, it is ultimately the humanity of Jesus that suffers the most. In the end, Jesus' victory—the victory of the spirit over flesh—is a victory over and renunciation of the physical body, the home, sex, marriage, work, children, and, perhaps most centrally, women. All these distinctly "unspiritual" sorts of things are instead portrayed as temptations to be resisted, thereby reinforcing the age-old stereotype that men are essentially spiritual and women are essentially sensuous and fleshly. It is true, of course, that Scorsese highlights the role of women in Jesus' movement, even going so far as to depict them at the Last Supper, "the only serious Jesus-film to allow this."[16] In the end, however, women are present in the Jesus story in order to seduce, tempt, and distract Jesus from his mission.

By trying to give us a human being wrestling with his "divine nature," Scorsese finally ends up with an individual who is really neither human nor divine. Following Kazantzakis, Scorsese begins with a dualism of flesh and spirit. Jesus then becomes the battle-ground in which those two opposing forces wage war. For the last two thousand years, however, this dualism has had disastrous conse-quences for christology. As long as flesh is viewed as belonging to a lower order and spirit to a higher one, not only is it impossible to affirm the Christian doctrine of creation (in which the flesh is es-sentially "good"), but the Christian doctrine of the incarnation in which we affirm that God has become flesh.

The Gospel According to St. Matthew (1966)

In 1962, Pier Paolo Pasolini, an avowed Marxist and atheist, stumbled across a Bible in his hotel room and, with time on his hands, began to read the gospels "from beginning to end, like a novel."[17] He was so struck by "the revolutionary quality"[18] of Matthew's Jesus that he decided to make a film using only the text of Matthew and without any of the extraneous material normally written into screenplays about Jesus for the sake of good storytelling. What Pasolini ends up with is nothing at all like the Hollywood Jesus-spectacles with their huge budgets, big-name actors, and elabo-rate sets. Filmed in black and white, in a stark, neo-realistic style, Pasolini used mostly nonprofessional actors and shot the scenes in remote locations in impoverished southern Italy. The faces of the actors (Pasolini uses frequent close-ups) are as rough and weatherworn as the landscapes. Except for Jesus, played by Enrique Irazoqui, the actors generally repeat their lines with little interpre-tation or feeling. Pasolini clearly wants to present the text of Mat-thew as simply and with as little embellishment as possible.

With its deliberately choppy editing, the film, as with the gospel of Matthew itself, is essentially a succession of scenes without narrative transitions or dramatic structure. Pasolini provides no introduction or development of the characters and practically no dialogue between the characters other than the sparse exchanges present in the text of Matthew. He employs virtually none of the standard Hollywood conventions for depicting the interior life of the characters or causal connections that help explain what is happening. For example, walking down a road and barely stopping to make eye contact, Jesus utters the following words to a group of five farmers: "Repent, for the kingdom of heaven is at hand." The same is true with the calling of the twelve disciples. He utters their names and they follow him. Nothing is added that would explain their motivation or how Jesus first made contact with them. Pasolini does not attempt to explain the meaning of the gospel, but instead attempts to evoke that meaning artistically.

Pasolini's Jesus is almost always on the move. He is frequently filmed from behind, talking as he is walking, and from the perspective of the disciples trying to keep up with him. The disciples are likewise filmed from the perspective of Jesus looking back at them. Pasolini frequently uses a handheld camera, such as during the inquisition of Jesus by the elders in the temple courtyard. The camera lingers on the outskirts of the action, weaving in and out among the crowd, behind people's heads and with long shots of the trial as if the viewer were one of Jesus' disciples watching the action. This technique adds a sense of realism and authenticity to the depiction of Jesus.

Jesus' words in the film are often caustic and biting. He is certainly not the blue-eyed evangelist of love, harmony, and peace created by George Stevens, and he is much more self-confident and decisive than the confused Jesus of Scorsese. Instead this Jesus is a social critic who is often angry, rarely smiles, lashes out at the religious establishment, and is quite stern with his own disciples. It is tempting to account for this with reference to Pasolini's Marxism. Consider, for example, the words of Jesus that appear only in Matthew: "Do not think that I came to bring peace on the earth; I did not come to bring peace, but a sword" (10:34). Pasolini's own run-ins with the law over his publicly admitted homosexuality as well as his arrest and trial for his film *La ricotta*, which was perceived as blasphemous, would clearly endear such words to him.

At the same time, it is impossible to blame Pasolini entirely for the aggressive and confrontational Jesus of Matthew. It is difficult, in fact, to read through Matthew in a single sitting without coming away impressed by the fact that this Jesus does not fit in with his own social world. He is at odds with the pious, with the wealthy, with the scribes, Pharisees, Sadducees, and temple leadership, with the entire political establishment, with lawyers, with his hometown synagogue, and often with his own disciples. This Jesus even curses a fig tree because it has no fruit! Pasolini, however, takes this conflict far beyond the text of Matthew and isolates it as virtually the only dimension of Jesus' character (though Pasolini's Jesus is always affectionate and warm to children).

Is Pasolini's Jesus fully human and fully divine? It is difficult to say. The fact that the filmmaker is a nonbeliever did not prevent the film from being acclaimed by religious and secular critics alike as a "masterpiece" and perhaps the greatest Jesus film ever made. Because the film uses only the text of the gospels, it is rather difficult for a Christian to criticize the screenplay! And yet, as with the previous two films, there are elements in the film that undercut both the humanity and the divinity of Jesus. Pasolini, for example, does not include Peter's confession of faith in Christ, and most of the parables of the reign of God are completely missing from the film. Rarely does Jesus announce or model the reign of God; he typically confines himself to denouncing obstacles to that reign. At the same time, because of Jesus' physical and emotional distance from most of the other human beings in the film, his humanity is eroded or at least severely attenuated. The fiery prophet portrayed by Pasolini has no companionship or human relations. He strides across the Italian hillsides hurling explosive lines at anyone who will listen. He appears intolerant and solitary. Like Stevens' portrait, this Jesus is a "world renouncer,"[19] but in a confrontational rather than sentimental mode.

Perhaps we must finally conclude that it is impossible to make a good film about Jesus. Maybe it will always be the case that, whether through film or any other medium, a full assertion of the unique relationship of Jesus to God necessarily requires us to downplay his humanity, and vice versa. Perhaps we are forced into a trade-off between his holiness and his humanity.

Interestingly enough, in all three films the humanity and divinity of Jesus rise and fall together. All three offer us a Jesus who is not at home in the world and who therefore can be neither fully human nor the incarnation of a God who created the world. In other words, when Jesus' humanity is diminished, so also is his divinity. It is precisely *because* Jesus is the truly human one that we are able to see God so perfectly through him.

Unfortunately, we often use the word *human* in a pejorative sense. When we sin, we say that we are only "human." But theologically this is quite incorrect. Sin is a failure to be human; it is a departure from our God-created humanity. Jesus, who is tempted in everything like us but without sin, lays in front of us a path toward holiness that is, at the same time, a path toward becoming fully human. In trying to understand how Jesus can be both human and divine, we need not be forced into either a trade-off or a balance between the two. They stand or collapse together. In the person of Jesus, we come to see that holiness and humanity travel in the same direction.

QUESTIONS FOR DISCUSSION

1. Reflect on the film you have watched and evaluate its portrayal of Jesus. Does the film work as a faithful portrayal of Jesus?
2. How does the film portray the humanity of Jesus? Are you satisfied with that portrayal?
3. What about Jesus' divinity? Does the Jesus in this film appear to be the Messiah and Son of God?
4. Is it possible to portray Jesus' divinity and humanity at the same time, or are these contradictory qualities?

RELATED FILMS

Godspell (1973)
The Gospel Road (1973)
Hail Mary (1985)
Jesus Christ Superstar (1973)

Jesus of Nazareth (1977)
King of Kings (1961)
The King of Kings (1927)
The Messiah (1975)

NOTES

[1]Ephesians 2:8.

[2]These "Gnostics," who rejected the physical, earthly, and bodily as the proper sphere of salvation, were also called "Docetists" (from the Greek word *dokeo*, "to seem") because Jesus, for them, only "seemed" to be human. Because of his divine nature, they argued, Jesus did not actually participate in the full human condition. For some Docetists this was even taken to the extreme of claiming that Jesus never blinked or left footprints!

[3]C. E. B. Cranfield, *The Apostles' Creed* (Grand Rapids, Mich.: Eerdmans, 1993), 30; Jennings, *Loyalty to God*, 95–96; Marthaler, *The Creed*, 124.

[4]It is even said that in production, Von Sydow was not allowed to smoke in front of the other actors! "Forget the Incense," *Time* (December 28, 1962), 35.

[5]Fred Myers, "We Kid You Not!" *Christian Century* 82 (April 21, 1965), 492.

[6]Ibid.

[7]For example, the film conflates Lazarus with the rich young man, identifies Mary Magdalene as the woman caught in adultery, and has Judas throw himself into the sacrificial fire on the temple grounds instead of hanging himself.

[8]According to W. Barnes Tatum, "More than any other Jesus film, *The Greatest Story Ever Told* moves under the influence of the gospel of John." *Jesus at the Movies*, 94.

[9]"Forget the Incense," 35.

[10]Quoted by Tatum, *Jesus at the Movies*, 89.

[11]Baugh, *Imaging the Divine*, 31.

[12]Ibid., 54.

[13]According to Roger Ebert, "This scene is shot with such restraint and tact that it does not qualify in any way as a 'sex scene,' but instead is simply an illustration of marriage and the creation of children," *Chicago Sun-Times*, August 12, 1988.

[14]Tatum, *Jesus at the Movies*, 163.

[15]Martin Scorsese, quoted by Kenneth von Gunden, *Postmodern Auteurs: Coppola, Lucas, De Palma, Spielberg, and Scorsese* (Jefferson, N.C.: McFarland & Company, 1991), 159.

[16]Ibid.

[17]Quoted by Baugh, 94.

[18]Ibid.

[19]Ibid., 104.

6

"Suffered under Pontius Pilate"

 *Romero*

In his book *Honest to Jesus*, Robert Funk, one of the principal founders of the "Jesus Seminar,"[1] makes the point that the Apostles' Creed is a "creed with an empty center." In narrating Jesus' life, the creed leaps without explanation from Jesus' birth to his suffering under Pontius Pilate. Says Funk,

> It scarcely requires notice that this creed calls on the believer to affirm nothing about the historical Jesus other than his virgin birth at the beginning of his life and his suffering, execution, and resurrection at the end…the ethical dimensions of the gospels of both Jesus and Paul have been lost in the creedal formulation: believers only have to believe; they are not required to modify their behavior in any other respect.[2]

Funk's complaint must be taken seriously. It is possible to so preoccupy ourselves with high claims for Jesus' deity and lordship or with specific events in Jesus' life such as his birth, passion, or resurrection that we neglect what Jesus actually taught and how Jesus actually called us to live. So, for example, while Jesus proclaimed the reign of God and modeled the kind of relationships and allegiances that characterize that reign, the church from very early on began instead to proclaim Jesus himself. Less than two months after Jesus' death, Peter's entire sermon at Pentecost

(Acts 2:14–36) is devoted to proclaiming Jesus' identity as Messiah and Lord. Nothing, however, is said about Jesus' "Way"—his values, associations, commitments—or the requirements he set for those who would be his disciples. In other words, "the message *of* Jesus became a message *about* Jesus."[3]

It is not difficult, therefore, to see how a creed can become a substitute for the gospel or how an evangelism that invites others to accept Jesus as Messiah, Son of God, and Lord can actually function as a tool for emptying Jesus' radical "Way" of its offense and scandal. As liberation theologian Juan Luis Segundo says,

> There is no longer any need to know whether people's values fit in with those of the kingdom, however primitively and gradually. The only question now is whether they do or do not recognize Jesus as the Messiah of Israel. The former could take a matter of months or years to answer, and it could entail concrete manifestations. The latter question is answered in a matter of seconds or minutes.[4]

Perhaps it is possible, however, to combine the proclamation *of* Jesus and the proclamation *about* Jesus so that they are one seamless proclamation rather than two different proclamations. There is a phrase in the creed that may help us link these two together and perhaps even fill the "empty center" to which Robert Funk refers. Oddly enough, it is the phrase "suffered under Pontius Pilate." Upon close examination, this single phrase is not only a statement about a particular event in Jesus' life, but one that presupposes a claim about the content of his life and teachings. To make the claim that Jesus was betrayed, interrogated, tortured, ridiculed, and crucified, we are forced to consider the values, relationships, and allegiances that led to such treatment. Jesus' suffering and death cannot be understood apart from the "Way" that led to them.[5]

It may be somewhat surprising that Pontius Pilate, an otherwise largely unknown governor of Judea (C.E. 26–36), would be mentioned so strikingly in what has come to serve as the formative creed of Christianity. In fact, he is one of only two names mentioned other than Jesus himself (Mary, as we have seen, is the other). Why does Pilate figure so prominently in a Christian's affirmation of loyalty to Jesus? For one thing, the reference to Pilate is an assertion of the historical nature of Christian salvation by dating it within human history. In this way, the creed locates the origins of Christian faith "not in myth and legend, but in the sphere of human history, the sphere of war and conquest, of intrigue and dominion, of power politics and imperial force."[6]

Not only does this reference to Pilate provide a historical context for Jesus' suffering and death, it provides a political context as well. This it does by linking the passion of Jesus to the concrete structures of domination and oppression in his day. Jesus' "Way" and the salvation he makes possible, we learn, have political implications and consequences. Sin and evil are rarely only personal or interpersonal realities; they have a systemic nature that operates through public institutions like governments, corporations, or even religious bodies. To take seriously the kind of faith called for by Jesus, therefore, is eventually to find oneself in the sphere of the political.

Oscar Romero: Faith and Politics

It is precisely this intersection of faith and politics that the film *Romero* (1989) seeks to portray in the life, transformation, and martyrdom of Archbishop Oscar Romero of El Salvador. *Romero* was produced by an agency of the Paulist Fathers, a religious order of Roman Catholic missionaries and communicators in North America. As the first commercial feature film ever produced under church-based auspices,[7] *Romero* is not a typical "Hollywood" movie. In fact, all three major television networks turned down the project as "too depressing," "too controversial," and lacking in "love interest."[8] Ellwood Kieser, producer of the film and himself a Paulist priest, described the film as "an act of evangelism."[9] As Margaret Miles notes, however, *Romero* does not avoid many of the standard film conventions of Hollywood "adventure films" such as, for example, the depiction of "a hero whose character develops while the characters of those surrounding him remain static" or the casting of several young women "as foils for the male protagonist's struggles."[10] Still, the film has been described as "a labor of love," with most of the actors working for the union minimum and lead actor Raul Julia accepting one-seventh of his usual salary for his starring role.[11] In fact, Julia, who described himself in an interview as having been "a lapsed Catholic," claimed to have had something of a conversion during the filming that rekindled his faith. Said Julia, "What impressed me the most about Romero is that he saw the people who came to his church as the church. The church was not an intellectual matter for him, it was a living experience."[12]

Oscar Romero was appointed archbishop of war-torn El Salvador in 1977, more than likely because of his centrist position in the

Romero: © Four Seasons Entertainment, Inc., Courtesy MoMA

church. Though widely recognized as a good priest, a sound theologian, and a solid proponent of social justice and reform, he was also known as a sharp critic of the more radical theologies surfacing throughout Central and Latin America. As two of the more conservative bishops in the film agree, "He's a good compromise choice; he'll make no waves. He's a bookworm. The whole country could be running wild; he wouldn't even notice it." But, in fact, Romero did notice; indeed, a number of events in his first weeks as archbishop, several of them depicted in the film, were a catalyst for bringing about dramatic change in his ideas, loyalties, and commitments.[13]

Romero became archbishop during El Salvador's twelve-year-long civil war, which claimed the lives of more than sixty thousand Salvadoran civilians, an estimated 85 percent of them at the hands of the military and right-wing "death squads."[14] While the nation of El Salvador was being torn apart both from within and without, so also was the Salvadoran church. On the one hand, the institutional church had become a lackey to the interests of the wealthy ruling elite and the military. The church's official stance of political neutrality had, in effect, become an instrument of the status quo. As Desmond Tutu, Anglican archbishop of South Africa, puts it, "If you are neutral in a situation of injustice, you have chosen the side of the oppressor. If an elephant has his foot on the tail of the mouse, and you say you are neutral, the mouse will not appreciate your neutrality."[15]

On the other hand, a significant group of priests and theologians within the church espoused what has come to be known as "liberation theology," a movement that emphasizes the solidarity of Christ with the poor and accentuates the political, even revolutionary, implications of Christ's gospel. Romero's good friend, Father Rutilio Grande, represents this view in the film, just as he did in real life.[16] At one point he says to his companion priests, "Pretty soon they won't allow the Bible into our country any more. All we'll get is the bindings because everything inside, all the pages, will be declared revolutionary." In many cases, these priests and theologians found themselves working elbow to elbow with Marxists who were also working to organize the poor in a grassroots movement to bring about reforms and overthrow the totalitarian government. For this reason—and also because some liberation theologians actually employed elements of Marxist social analysis (without Marx's atheism)—these more radical priests were accused of being "communists" by the governing powers in both El Salvador and in the United States. This label thereby helped to justify government and military sponsored repression not only of all economic and land reform movements, but also of the church itself. It also helped secure military and financial aid from the United States as a way of fighting a communism that was perceived to be infiltrating throughout Central and Latin America.

This larger conflict within Salvadoran culture and within the church eventually became a conflict within Romero himself. Though the film version of Romero's life attempts to portray this inner conflict, it tends to be minimized on screen because of the stark contrast that is painted between good and evil all around him.[17] Throughout the film, Romero's course of action is rarely anything other than predictable, though there are some moments of suspense, and clearly Romero is presented as an individual being transformed by having his eyes opened to reality.

When Romero is first appointed archbishop, he tries not to inflame the situation he has inherited: "The Church must keep to the center watchfully, in the traditional way, but seeking justice." He warns the more radical priests about being "sub…subversive" (he can barely pass this offensive word through his lips). One after another, however, Romero sees his own priests being murdered along with the poor whom they serve. Romero the "bookworm" becomes Romero the "prophet," and he begins to understand the subversive and unsettling message of Christ in a world of injustice and oppression. Romero, who was once concerned that the message of the church not be perceived as in any way incendiary can now proclaim boldly, "The mission of the church is to identify itself with the poor and to join with them in their struggle for justice. By so doing, the church finds its own salvation." On the Sunday prior to his assassination, Romero pleaded with members of the military to disobey killing orders that were contrary to their religious and moral convictions. He spoke out to all those with power in the country, "I implore you, I beg you, I order you, stop the repression!" He was shot two days later while saying mass in the chapel of the cancer hospital where he lived.

Romero is popularly thought of throughout the world today as a saint (and his eventual canonization as a matter of "when," not "if"). In fact, it might seem plausible to draw an analogy between Christ and Romero and between Pontius Pilate and the oppressive Salvadoran regime. In several scenes this analogy is underscored, as when Romero is stripped to his waist and mocked by soldiers. Also supportive of such an interpretation are words spoken by Romero in a phone interview just two weeks prior to his murder:

> I have often been threatened with death. I must tell you, as a Christian, I do not believe in death without resurrection. If I am killed, I shall arise in the Salvadoran people. I say so without boasting, with the greatest humility.

> As a shepherd, I am obliged by divine mandate to give my life for those I love—for all Salvadorans, even for those who may be going to kill me. If the threats are carried out, from

this moment I offer my blood to God for the redemption and for the resurrection of El Salvador.

Martyrdom is a grace of God that I do not believe I deserve. But if God accepts the sacrifice of my life, let my blood be a seed of freedom and the sign that hope will soon be a reality. Let my death, if it is accepted by God, be for my people's liberation and as a witness of hope in the future.

You may say, if they succeed in killing me, that I pardon and bless those who do it. Would, indeed, that they might be convinced that they will waste their time. A bishop will die, but God's church, which is the people, will never perish.[18]

Though Romero's words here might support our viewing him as a Christ-figure, the more consistent theme in Romero's homilies and radio broadcasts is that it is the poor who are the church and who should properly be understood collectively as a Christ-figure, as in his words taken from the film:

You have not suffered alone, for you are the church. You are the people of God. You are Jesus in the here and now. He is crucified in you, just as surely as he was crucified 2,000 years ago on that hill outside of Jerusalem. And you should know that your pain and your suffering, like his, will contribute to El Salvador's liberation and redemption.

For Romero, it is the poor who today suffer under Pontius Pilate and in whom Christ is to be found. Indeed, Romero eventually came to believe that the church must make "a preferential option for the poor."[19] Just one week prior to his assassination, Romero expressed the view that the poor and the oppressed "besides being human beings, are also divine beings, since Jesus said that whatever is done to them he takes as done to him."[20]

Romero's solidarity with the poor, the families of the "disappeared," and those who suffered under government and military repression led him increasingly to understand his faith as having political consequences. Throughout his life, however, he consistently expressed an ambivalent attitude toward any easy alliance between faith and politics. On the one hand, for Romero, violence, bloodshed, and death must be understood within a political framework. On the other hand, insofar as "they touch the very heart of God," violence, bloodshed and death are "beyond all politics."[21] On the day before his assassination, Romero expressed hope for "better land distribution, a better financial system for the country, a political arrangement better suited for the common good of the citizens." But in the same breath he located this hope in "the context of definitive liberation" and states that "God's program to liberate the people is a transcendent one."[22]

Romero's synthesis may prove helpful for our own attempt to understand the relationship between faith and politics. Romero understands that Christian salvation occurs on the plane of the political and that as Christians we must immerse ourselves in the world. He understands that economic injustice is at the root of the violence in El Salvador. He even takes it upon himself to write a letter to the President of the United States, asking that no more arms be sent to his country. At the same time, Romero is wary of reducing the Christian life to a set of merely political solutions, something he calls "political opportunism."[23] According to Romero, "Christian love goes beyond all categories of regimes and systems. The church is not identified with any political system. The church cannot identify itself with any political organization."[24]

This synthesis should not be construed as "balance," "compromise," or finding a position that is "middle-of-the road." It is out of concern to preserve the radical and liberating nature of the gospel that Romero refuses to allow Christian faith to be reduced to any one political faction or solution. In this sense the gospel both *is* and *is not* subversive:

> Let not the church's mission of evangelizing and working for justice be confused with subversive activities. It is very different—unless the gospel is to be called subversive, because it does indeed touch the foundations of an order that should not exist, because it is unjust.[25]

There are a number of similarities between Romero and Jesus of Nazareth at this point. Jesus refused to identify himself with any particular political program, whether of the Sadducees on the right or the Zealots on the left. But this does not mean that Jesus was nonpolitical. To side with the poor and the marginalized of society in a situation where poverty and marginalization are rooted and sustained in a political system is quite certainly to be political—and subversively so. It is often thought that because Jesus did not direct his energies against Roman authority he was therefore not political. But this misses the primary context of political intrigue, speculation, and controversy in which Jesus was embroiled daily throughout his ministry. The immediate political leadership of Jesus' day was to be found in the religious establishment, which included the scribes, priests, and elders, factions such as the Pharisees, Sadducees, and Herodians, and a tribunal known as the Sanhedrin. On page after page of all four gospels, Jesus defies and systematically alienates these brokers of religious and political power by directing his sermons and parables against their authority, views, and practices. No one escapes criticism.

Not only were Jesus' life and teachings political, so also were his sufferings and death, as the Apostles' Creed asserts through its reference to Pilate. To read the New Testament accounts of the sufferings of Jesus is to read about the sufferings of a political prisoner. The entire narrative is teeming with late-night council meetings, backroom deals, abuse from soldiers, imprisonment, false witnesses, trials, torture, and capital punishment. According to Jennings,

> The degree to which this is strange or foreign to us is the measure of how far we are from a simple and obedient attention to the plainest assertions of Bible and Creed. We don't want to speak of governors and soldiers, of the political and military sphere. We would often prefer to speak of a suffering that is thoroughly "religious" or "spiritual" rather than political.[26]

But by doing so, we cut ourselves off from reality—both the historical reality recorded in the New Testament and our own present reality in which, as Romero knew, faith must be lived politically or not at all.

Pilate was not Jesus' enemy. He was not out to get Jesus. In fact, the gospels are much less harsh in their assessment of Pilate than are other ancient Jewish sources of the same period,[27] perhaps because Pilate testifies to the "innocence" of Jesus and was even ready to release him. And yet the reference to Pilate in the Apostles' Creed demonstrates how politically entrenched are structures that thwart *shalom* and justice, especially for the poor. It also shows how politically dangerous a simple man with a simple message can be.[28] Pilate probably knew well how to "win friends and influence people." He simply chose the route of expediency. He probably did little more than allow his top political advisors to cut a deal with an important constituency in his jurisdiction to ensure his own political survival, preserve peace, and quash a popular uprising behind one of many "messiahs" who appeared from time to time throughout the ancient Near East.

What the creed points to and what we see plainly in *Romero* is that there can be no division between the spiritual and the political. Try as we may to avoid the political, even this avoidance is a political choice to allow things to remain the same—and in the end, that is a spiritual choice. Loyalty to the one who suffered under Pontius Pilate requires a faith that refuses to shrink back from a world of injustice and that willingly shares in his sufferings as it sides with the lowly and disinherited who, as Romero reminded us, are themselves Christ crucified in our own time.

> The Church, entrusted with the earth's glory, believes that in each person is the creator's image and that everyone who tramples it offends God…The Church takes as spittle in its face, as lash on its back, as the cross in its passion, all that human beings suffer, even though they be unbelievers. They suffer as God's images. There is no dichotomy between [humanity] and God's image. Whoever tortures a human being, whoever abuses a human being, whoever outrages a human being, abuses God's image, and the Church takes as its own that cross, that martyrdom.[29]

QUESTIONS FOR DISCUSSION

1. Are there qualities in Romero's life and ministry that you think are analogous to Christ's life and ministry?
2. Was Jesus "political"?
3. Should the church be "political"?
4. Pontius Pilate seems like an odd choice to be included in something as important as the Apostles' Creed. Why do you think he is included?

RELATED FILMS

Boyz N the Hood (1991)
Schindler's List (1993)
Shadowlands (1993)
Shoah (1985)
Sophie's Choice (1982)
Steel Magnolias (1989)

NOTES

[1]The controversial "Jesus Seminar" is an ongoing society of more than 200 biblical scholars created in 1985 as an attempt to determine with as much accuracy as possible the authenticity of Jesus' words and deeds in the gospels.

[2]Robert W. Funk, *Honest to Jesus: Jesus for a New Millennium* (San Francisco: Harper & Row, 1996), 43.

[3]Juan Luis Segundo, *The Christ of the Ignatian Exercises*, trans. John Drury (Maryknoll, N.Y.: Orbis Books, 1987), 19.

[4]Ibid.

[5]Cranfield notes that John Calvin's *Geneva Catechism* of 1541 asks why the creed goes immediately from the birth of Jesus to his death, passing over the whole history of his life. The answer: "Because nothing is said here [in the creed] but what pertains properly to the substance of our redemption." Cranfield agrees with Karl Barth (*Dogmatics in Outline*, 1949, 101ff.) that this is an entirely unsatisfactory answer, since it is the whole of Jesus' life (and not just his birth and death) that reveals who God is and provides for us the way of life. As Cranfield says, "The suffering that reached its fearful climax in the Passion characterized the whole of his life," *The Apostles' Creed*, 32.

[6]Jennings, *Loyalty to God*, 98.

[7]Jim Rice, "A Labor of Love and Truth," *Sojourners* (November 1989): 24.

[8]Ibid

[9]Stephan Ulstein, "Celluloid Evangelism," *Christianity Today* (November 3, 1989): 78

[10]Miles, *Seeing and Believing*, 64.

[11]Rice, 24.

[12]Ibid., 25.

[13]James R. Brockman, *Romero: A Life* (Maryknoll, N.Y.: Orbis Books, 1989), 61.

[14]Dean Peerman, "*Romero*: Evolution of a Martyr," *Christian Century* (October 4, 1989): 871.

[15]Quoted by Robert McAfee Brown, *Unexpected News: Reading the Bible with Third World Eyes* (Philadelphia: Westminster Press, 1984), 19.

[16]James R. Brockman, *The Word Remains: A Life of Oscar Romero* (Maryknoll, N.Y.: Orbis Books, 1983), 9.

[17]It should be noted, however, that many familiar with this period in El Salvador's history have defended the film as realistic and even understated in its toned-down depiction of state-sponsored repression. Rice, 25.

[18]Quoted by Brockman, *Romero: A Life*, 248.

[19]"I am glad, brothers and sisters, that our church is persecuted precisely for its preferential option for the poor and for trying to become incarnate on behalf of the poor." Quoted in *The Church Is All of You: Thoughts of Archbishop Oscar Romero*, comp. and trans. James R. Brockman (Minneapolis: Winston Press, 1984), 90.

[20]Ibid., 107; cf. Matthew 25: 31–46.

[21]Ibid.

[22]Ibid., 109.

[23]Ibid., 100.

[24]Ibid., 72.

[25]Ibid., 93.

[26]Jennings, 101.

[27]Marthaler, *The Creed*, 143.

[28]For another example of this truth, see the film *Gandhi* (1982).

[29]Quoted in Brockman, *The Church is All of You*, 20.

7

"Was crucified, died, and was buried. He descended to the dead."

 *One Flew Over the Cuckoo's Nest*

If the cross is the central symbol of Christianity, it is also its central scandal. For almost two thousand years, Christians have claimed that a Jewish teacher from a remote town on the eastern rim of the Mediterranean began to travel from town to town preaching and performing healings. As his following grew, he eventually drew the attention and consternation of the powerful. During the highest holy season, in the crowded city of Jerusalem, a strategy of deception and misinformation was orchestrated by these powers, setting in motion a chain of events involving a setup, a betrayal, and his arrest on charges of disturbing the peace. The man was handed over to the authorities, who pronounced a quick sentence of capital punishment by crucifixion.

Historically, there was nothing unique about this man's death. Crucifixion was a daily occurrence and but one in an arsenal of sadistic punishments the Romans were known to have inflicted on their enemies or on those who would disturb the *pax Romana*, the "peace of Rome." The first-century historian Josephus writes that during the sack of Jerusalem (66–70 C.E.), the Romans beat, tortured, and then crucified so many Jewish rebels—sometimes as many as five hundred per day—that the Romans had difficulty finding enough crosses or space to put them.

What makes the crucifixion of this man so scandalous, then, is not its historical peculiarity, but rather the subsequent claim by Christians that his crucifixion is somehow "good news" that makes possible a liberated and authentic life today, two thousand years later. How is this possible? And how do we reconstruct the full theological significance of the phrase "he was crucified, died, and was buried" when the only crosses we see do not bear fresh blood stains but are instead sanitized, lit up in neon, or molded into plastic? Like the early Christians, the sight of crosses is for us also a daily occurrence, but the crosses we are likely to see adorn the tops of ornate houses of worship or are cast in 24-carat gold and pinned to the noses of punk rockers.

The cross has come a long way indeed. What was originally an inhumane, torturous form of execution by the state has now become detached from its original historical setting and been made a part of our wider culture. Unfortunately, this makes the job of reconstructing the meaning of the cross all the more difficult for us today.

If we explore the cinematic usage of the cross, we do not always find much help. It is certainly possible to find examples of the cross on steeples or worn as ornaments in key movie scenes; often a cross can carry considerable symbolic freight in a film. Perhaps the most prominent use of the cross is to be found in horror films where a crucifix is used to protect against vampires and as a weapon to fight off evil. If a film wants to exaggerate the presence of evil, it can even feature desecrations of the cross as in *The Exorcist* (1973), or portray it in effigy as in *The Final Conflict* (1981).

When it comes to cinematic versions of the actual crucifixion of Jesus, virtually all the Jesus films feature some dramatization of the event, though these vary with regard to how much reality is incorporated. In most of the classic Hollywood films, the crucifixion is clean, quick, and relatively nonviolent, with a minimum of bloodshed. In *The Greatest Story Ever Told*, for example, the crucifixion is filmed using frequent long shots to avoid too graphic a representation, and in *The Messiah*, director Roberto Rossellini avoids any dramatization at all of Jesus' beating, torture, or forced carrying of the cross along the *via crucis*. In many of these films, there are even heavenly choirs singing in the background rather than the screams and moans one might expect. There are, of course, those few films that do not shrink back from the violence of the crucifixion. Indeed, *The Last Temptation of Christ*, directed by Martin Scorsese, revels in the sheer brutality of the cross, employing there and elsewhere in the film generous quantities of blood, a device that has become something of a Scorsese trademark.[1]

In most of the standard Jesus films, however, it is not immediately apparent why or how the crucifixion of Jesus is somehow liberating either for those standing by or for those of us who live two thousand years later. In fact, it could be easily argued that explicit portrayals of Jesus' crucifixion may actually be one of the least powerful means for communicating the significance of the cross today. Because such representations often serve hagiographic interests (sometimes Jesus even gets a halo while on the cross) and because the story of Jesus is disconnected from our own contemporary struggles and projects, Jesus' death on the cross is treated as a distant historical event merely to be replayed visually.

There are, however, films wherein a Christ-figure—one whose life and experience serve as a metaphor for Christ—can actually communicate the significance of the cross more powerfully than a historical reenactment of the event. In fact, what typically constitutes a Christ-figure as Christ-figure is some form of metaphorical crucifixion—the suffering, if not the death, of the protagonist for the redemption and liberation of others. Often, this occurs on screen with some sort of physical representation of a cross nearby or worn, as in the case of *The Passion of Joan of Arc (1928)*, *La ricotta*, *Babette's Feast* (1987), or *The Navigator: A Medieval Odyssey* (1988). A character's body can also take a cruciform pose in key scenes.[2] In *Braveheart*, for example, the legendary hero William Wallace is stretched out on a rack with arms outspread physically in the form of a cross. In other films, while there is no physical representation of a cross, the death or sacrifice of the Christ-figure is still a powerful symbol of crucifixion.

In the history of cinema, Jack Nicholson is, without a doubt, the most unlikely of Christ-figures. His devilish eyebrows, diabolic grin, mischievous eyes, and fiendish laugh all combine to make him more of a sinner than a saint. In Miloš Forman's *One Flew Over the*

Cuckoo's Nest (1975), however, Nicholson is brilliant as the Christ-figure who stands up against the forces of evil and domination and whose life and death serve as a means of redemption and liberation for his fellow patients. The film is surely one of the great achievements of American cinema. An adaptation of Ken Kesey's classic

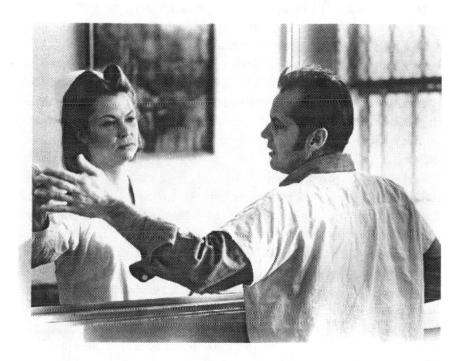

One Flew Over the Cuckoo's Nest: © Fantasy Films and United Artists Corporation, Courtesy MoMA

novel by the same name, *One Flew over the Cuckoo's Nest* is only the second movie ever to have swept all five of the top Oscars (Best Picture, Best Director, Best Actor, Best Actress, and Best Screenplay).

Nicholson plays the role of Randall Patrick ("R. P.") McMurphy, a troublemaking convict who has been faking insanity in order to get transferred from a prison work farm to a psychiatric ward for observation and treatment. When McMurphy arrives, he dances around happily and even kisses the security guard, believing he has entered the promised land. Instead, he enters a world that is dominated by the manipulative Nurse Ratched (Louise Fletcher), whose placid smile is a thin veneer over her passive-aggressive style of intimidation and control. The patients in the ward are a motley group of both the sane and insane, many of whom have committed themselves voluntarily in order to hide from personal despair or the pressures of family and society. Included among the patients are Billy, a shy, stuttering, young paranoid who has issues that stem back to fear of his mother; Martini, a man with the personality of a child; Harding, an arrogant man who, though saner than the others, cannot get over his wife's infidelity; Cheswick, an insecure neurotic who is easily reduced to tears or fits of screaming; and "Chief" Bromden, a tall Native American who is (or at least claims to be) both deaf and mute. The film is strengthened considerably by the performances of these and other patients and by the appearance in the background of another group of men, the "chronics," who have virtually no interactive skills, some of whom were played in the film by actual patients.

McMurphy introduces anarchy and chaos into Nurse Ratched's tightly controlled world as he begins to infect his fellow patients with a sense of dignity and a thirst for freedom. In essence, he leads a rebellion against her authority and regulations. Starting with subtle mind games (captured brilliantly on screen through a powerful use of close-ups), McMurphy engages Nurse Ratched in a contest of wills as he challenges the rigid set of rules by which the patients are organized and controlled. The battle between McMurphy and Nurse Ratched gradually takes on larger proportions, eventually becoming a struggle between good and evil, dignity and humiliation, liberation and oppression.

Nurse Ratched and the "Domination System"

In his acclaimed *Powers* trilogy,[3] Walter Wink calls attention to the reality of ruthless systems and structures in the world—invisible and pervasive powers that over time come to have a life of their own. Though these oppressive forces dominate our lives, they are not easily identifiable or reducible to single causes; they seem to conspire together in a systematic attempt to thwart human freedom, community, justice, and peace. Wink calls this overarching network of powers the "Domination System."

> [The Domination System] is characterized by unjust economic relations, oppressive political relations, biased race relations, patriarchal gender relations, hierarchical power

relations, and the use of violence to maintain them all. No matter what shape the dominating system of the moment might take (from the ancient Near Eastern states to the Pax Romana to feudal Europe to communist state capitalism to modern market capitalism), the basic structure has persisted now for at least five thousand years.[4]

This is not to say that sin and evil only exist outside of us as forces that are alien to us; rather, our complicity with the powers of domination is what sustains them and even brings them into being. As Wink says, "Their evil is not intrinsic, but the result of idolatry."[5] And yet, the domination system readily takes on its own independent, demonic personality. The key to finding liberation from the domination system and, indeed, to pursuing its redemption is to understand the mechanisms by which it achieves its hold on our lives. Only by first exposing the myths by which they keep us as humans working for our own destruction can the powers be confronted, defeated, and even transformed.

One Flew Over the Cuckoo's Nest may be viewed as something of a case study in the working dynamics of the domination system. Nurse Ratched is, of course, the symbol of its power and of the brutal mechanisms of domination. Her calm exterior can barely hide the anger and hostility that lie below its surface as she perpetuates a system of control and intimidation to which the patients have passively allowed themselves to become enslaved. She does not need to use force. She reigns over a polished system of institutional policies and procedures to which the individual will is subjected and thereby dominated.

At one point in the film, for example, McMurphy proposes during group therapy that the work detail be rearranged to accommodate watching the opening game of the World Series on television. Nurse Ratched informs him that it would not be a good idea to alter the ward's "carefully worked out schedule." "Some men on the ward," she explains, "take a long, long time to get used to the schedule. Change it now, and they might find it very disturbing." She allows the matter to come to a vote, however, but McMurphy's cause attracts only three votes. Ratched knows the patients have a fear of freedom and will willingly allow themselves to remain slaves of the system. Indeed, one of the most formidable mechanisms of the domination system is its capacity for subjugating the individual to an allegedly higher good—the system itself—which, in this case, takes the form of Nurse Ratched's "ward policy."

Following the vote, however, McMurphy confronts the patients in the tub-room about their passivity and offers his first summons to freedom. He claims he will escape from the hospital and go watch the World Series downtown in a bar. "Anybody want to come with me?" he asks. McMurphy makes a wager that he can smash his way out of the ward by lifting a heavy marble sink and throwing it through one of the barred windows. In an emotionally charged scene, McMurphy struggles and strains to lift the sink, grimacing and groaning until his face is flushed red—and in that moment one gets the impression that McMurphy is actually struggling against the entire weight of the domination system itself. The sink is much too heavy, however, and he is forced to give up. Rather than admit defeat, however, he leaves the room defiantly for at least having tried.

The next day, McMurphy is able to talk Nurse Ratched into taking a second vote, and this time he succeeds in swinging all nine of the group members' votes. Nurse Ratched finds a new way of thwarting his idea, however, and informs McMurphy that a majority vote must take into account the additional nine men on the ward, the "chronics," who do not participate in group therapy and who have little or no rational ability. McMurphy cannot believe his ears. He still needs one more vote. As McMurphy moves from one man to the next, trying to get at least one of them to raise his hand, Nurse Ratched declares the meeting adjourned. Finally, "Chief" Bromden slowly raises his hand as McMurphy breaks into shouts of celebration only to find out that Nurse Ratched refuses to recognize what has happened. "When the meeting was adjourned the vote was nine to nine," she insists. The domination system, which finds its destructive incarnation in the person of Nurse Ratched, "plays with a stacked deck," as McMurphy later objects.

The domination system is, of course, adept at cloaking its evil. We do not always on the surface of things perceive it as something wicked. Even Hitler's regime was not recognized at first for what it was, even by the most pious of individuals. The idolatrous powers of domination are almost always imperceptible and camouflaged in good. They work through well-meaning institutions that exist for reform, health, prosperity, and the common good. They can even take on an altogether religious nature—indeed, religions themselves are especially ferocious as domination systems. As Wink says, "What killed Jesus was not irreligion, but religion itself; not lawlessness, but precisely the Law; not anarchy, but the upholding of order."[6] One can even trace quasi-religious dimensions of the domination system as they surface in *One Flew Over the Cuckoo's Nest*. At one point, McMurphy is unable to talk to the other patients during a card game because the piped-in music on the ward is too loud. He enters the nurses' station to turn the volume down, thereby breaking one of Nurse Ratched's fundamental ordinances. The nurses' station is something like a "Holy of Holies"—the center of power and control whence regulations, medicine, and valuable commodities like cigarettes are dispensed. In one memorable scene, the men even line up at the nurses' station to receive their medication as if they were receiving holy eucharist. One of the men actually sticks out his tongue to receive the pill, and the nurse places it ceremoniously as if it were a communion wafer.

Perhaps the most vicious mechanism by which the domination system achieves its control is its ability to feed on and grow stronger by active resistance against it. Fighting directly against the powers of domination often makes them only more powerful because of their pervasiveness and built-in appeal to a more fundamental (even supernatural) authority from which they pretend to draw their legitimacy. Thus, the powers are able to convince us that rebellion against the domination system is the real evil and that resistance should be branded as deviance.[7] So, for example, whenever McMurphy or the others challenge the system, they are accused of being "upset" and are instructed to "calm down." According to the domination system, the real problem is with the one who resists.

Again, it is important to recognize that the domination system need not oppress through coercion. It manipulates by playing on our fears, insecurities, and past failures. This form of exploitation is never more obvious than when Nurse Ratched is interacting with young Billy, pressing him on insecurities that have resulted from his domineering mother. Billy's stuttering is the verbal expression of this intimidation. In the film's denouement, McMurphy, who has the opportunity to escape, decides to throw a wild, drunken party—a sort of "Last Supper" for the inmates. After bribing the night watchman, he sneaks Candy and her friend, Rose, into the hospital. Inevitably the entire ward is wrecked, including, most especially, the sacred space of the nurses' station, which is left in a shambles. Though McMurphy has the chance to leave, he stays behind so Billy can "have a date" with Candy. When Billy is discovered in bed with Candy the next morning, Nurse Ratched goes immediately to work, forcing him to "explain everything" and making him feel guilty about his enjoyment of sex: "Aren't you ashamed?" Billy answers (without stuttering), "No, I'm not." Nurse Ratched then begins to turn the knife, "You know, Billy, what worries me is how your mother's going to take this." Billy's stuttering resumes as he is pressed by Nurse Ratched to explain who was behind the previous evening's fiasco. He finally succumbs and, as a Judas-figure, gives McMurphy's name. But then comes a fit of frenzy, and ultimately the most deadly of the weapons of the domination system—death itself.

The "powers that be" do not kill Billy directly. Though the domination system finds its central expression in Nurse Ratched, it does not work merely through the instrumentation of a single person. The real power of the domination system lies not in its ability to coerce, but in its seductive ability to lure us into complicity with that system—in the way it works in and through us as we give allegiance to that which enslaves us. Billy commits suicide.

So it is, then, that in *One Flew Over the Cuckoo's Nest* the single most devastating discovery for McMurphy is that almost all the patients on the ward are voluntary, and, though they constantly complain, they can leave whenever they want. The perversity of systemic evil is not ultimately its power to dominate through direct violence and victimization, but in its subtle way of enticing us into working against our very selves. This dynamic is expressed most poignantly when "Chief" Bromden opens up about his father to McMurphy.

> *Chief*: My poppa was real big. He did as he pleased. That's why they worked on him. The last time I saw my pa, he was blind and diseased from drinking. And when he held the bottle to his mouth, he don't suck out of it, it sucked out of him till he shriveled up so small that the dogs don't even know him.

McMurphy: They killed him?

Chief: I'm not saying they killed him. They just worked on him. The way they're working on you.

The Liberating Victory of the Cross

Is there a way out of the domination system? Is there a path toward liberation and dignity, toward the recovery of our authentic humanity? Can the powers symbolized so aptly in *One Flew Over the Cuckoo's Nest*, the powers that enslave and control, be conquered? For Christian faith, the answer to these questions is found centrally in the meaning of the crucifixion of Jesus. Thus, even though the phrase "was crucified" is but one in a list of events that the creed claims occurred in Jesus' life, the crucifixion has a centrality and priority that is unparalleled.

This does not mean that the cross can be isolated from the whole of Jesus' life and teachings. It is precisely his proclamation and his practice that led him to the cross. Nor does it mean that the crucifixion can be separated from the resurrection. Easter vindicates the life and mission of Jesus and breaks the power of death exposed by the cross. And yet, Christians have always found it essential to affirm the New Testament claim that "Christ died for our sins" (1 Cor. 15:3). The cross, therefore, is referred to by Christians as the "atonement" (literally "at-one-ment")—a provision of the way for humans to be reconciled to God. But the question remains, exactly how does Jesus' death accomplish this provision? Does the crucifixion change God? Or does it perhaps change us? Does Christ's death appease God's anger and satisfy God's demand for justice so that we are now able to approach God? Or does the death of Jesus instead reveal what God is always like—a loving Father who stands always ready to accept us with arms outstretched, the only condition being that we turn around and come home? A dialogue with *One Flew Over the Cuckoo's Nest* may prove helpful in trying to answer this question. Let us first, however, consider some of the more traditional ways in which the Christian tradition has approached this critically important issue.

Certainly the church's predominant way of answering this question, at least since the Middle Ages, has been the view that interpreted Jesus' death within the context of the ancient Jewish sacrificial system, specifically the bloody sacrifices prescribed for the forgiveness of sins. Given the fact that the New Testament was written largely from a Jewish perspective, it is not surprising that there is significant biblical support for such an interpretation. Jesus is referred to as a lamb that is sacrificed for our salvation—a "propitiation"[8] offering handed over to satisfy God's justice and wrath and to achieve our forgiveness. Sometimes called the "satisfaction" theory of the atonement, this view understands Jesus to be performing a substitutionary role in the drama of salvation. Jesus pays the debt that we owe and receives the penalty that we deserve. God is the one who needs to be "satisfied" for redemption to take place.

At the same time, the notion that a scapegoat is sufficient or required to let us sinners off the hook is not without its criticism— and, indeed, much of this criticism comes from within the Bible itself. When we look, for example, at the rich prophetic tradition in the Hebrew Scriptures—a tradition in which Jesus himself stands— we find a profound mistrust of the sacrificial system that should cause us to think twice about interpreting Jesus' death as a sacrifice.[9] Quoting the prophet Hosea, Jesus says, "I desire compassion and not sacrifice."[10] Thus, though Jesus' death is frequently interpreted in the New Testament by way of the sacrificial motif, we should be cautious about too easily understanding his sacrifice along the standard lines of the scapegoat theory. In fact, as the epistle to the Hebrews makes clear, Jesus is not to be understood as just any sacrifice, but as the sacrifice to end all sacrifices (Heb. 10:12)—the one who exposes the very inadequacy of the entire sacrificial system. We should not be surprised, then, to find Jesus going out of his way to attack the temple system and its power to reinforce the myth of redemptive violence. As Walter Wink notes, "Jesus' death...exposed and annulled the entire sacrificial system. His death ended temple slaughter and the necessity for sacred violence. Jesus' crucifixion laid bare the true nature of the sacrificial system, which projected the need for substitutionary slaughter into the very Godhead."[11]

However predominant the satisfaction theory of the atonement has become, there are other biblical ways of interpreting Jesus' crucifixion. A second popular interpretation of the atonement was put forward by the important medieval scholar Peter Abelard (1079–1142), who wrote that Christ's death was not so much a sacrifice to "satisfy" God's justice as it was a demonstration of God's reconciling love offered to win our hearts. As the apostle Paul says, "God demonstrates His own love toward us, in that while we were yet sinners, Christ died for us" (Rom. 5:8). Known as the *moral influence* theory of the atonement, this view holds that it is we rather than God who need to be changed. According to Abelard, we humans too often ignore God's long-suffering love, turning in on ourselves and becoming obsessed with personal ambitions. The cross is both the decisive manifestation of God's inexhaustible mercy toward us as well as an invitation for us to respond to our neighbor in turn with self-giving love and compassion. As 1 John 4:19 says, "We love, because He first loved us."

When we compare these two interpretations of the atonement—the satisfaction theory and the moral influence theory—we can see that the satisfaction theory tends to be more "objective." The broken relationship between God and humans must be restored by some gracious action outside of us that we cannot cause to happen and in which we have little involvement (other than, of course, trusting in and receiving its benefits). The moral influence theory, on the other hand, tends to be more "subjective"—reconciliation must centrally take place in us as humans, and thus the death of Christ is a profound influence that motivates us to turn around and head in a different direction. In the first, a change occurs outside of us. In the second, a change occurs within us.

There is, however, a third interpretation of Jesus' crucifixion—with considerable biblical and historical support—that is able to unite both the objective and subjective elements of the atonement and, at the same time, take into account the systemic nature of domination that we see manifested so vividly in *One Flew Over the Cuckoo's Nest*. Known as the "classical" or *Christus Victor* theory of the atonement, this interpretation holds that Christ's suffering and death on the cross are actually a battle against the powers of violence and oppression in which, remarkably, Christ is the victor. Contrary to external appearances, Christ is not being defeated by the powers of domination as he suffers their brutality and violence.

He is actually exposing them for what they are—he is ripping away the disguises by which they manipulate and dehumanize. As the apostle Paul says,

> He made you alive together with Him, having forgiven us all our transgressions, having canceled out the certificate of debt consisting of decrees against us and which was hostile to us; and He has taken it out of the way, having nailed it to the cross. When He had disarmed the rulers and authorities, He made a public display of them, having triumphed over them through Him. (Col. 2:13–15)

It is not the powers, but Jesus who is triumphing on the cross! It is Jesus who is nailing hostility and violence to the cross, putting an end to them! It is Jesus who is making a public display of the domination system! Even though this triumph takes place "objectively"—Jesus performs an act on our behalf—it also takes place "subjectively"—we are liberated as we come to see the truth about the powers and about our own complicity with those powers. The full implications of this triumph are profoundly holistic. Not only are we liberated from the powers, the powers themselves can be redeemed once the mechanisms of their oppression are exposed. As Wink notes, "The task of redemption is not restricted to changing individuals,...but also to changing their fallen institutions."[12]

What we see happening on the cross, then, is not some faraway act that magically appeases God's wrath, nor is it merely a powerful sermon that inspires us to turn to God or become better persons. It is an act that changes reality by exposing the domination system for what it is, and through that revelation—through Christ's innocent suffering—the myth of redemptive violence is negated and its power to enslave is broken. As a way of better allowing ourselves to be grasped by this mystery, let us consider further the way McMurphy's life and death can be viewed as a figure of Christ's atonement in *One Flew Over the Cuckoo's Nest*.

McMurphy, the Christ-Figure

Nurse Ratched, as focal symbol of the domination system, knows that she need not use force or coercion in order to enslave, dehumanize, and control the patients. Ironically, these forms of domination are actually very weak because they are relatively simple to expose and defeat. On the contrary, the most powerful way to control and dehumanize people is to get them to accept their situation as a "given" by appealing to a system of order, law, and social relations and by playing to basic human fears and insecurities.

By the same token, the most powerful way to liberate other people is not by directly attacking the powers that be, but by exposing them for what they are in the minds and hearts of those being dominated and dehumanized. McMurphy does not always understand this with regard to Nurse Ratched, and early on he goes after her head-on. And yet the power of *One Flew Over the Cuckoo's Nest* is its portrayal of McMurphy as the one who liberates his fellow patients by steadily summoning them to freedom and dignity. McMurphy is an unlikely redeemer who calls the men to be fully human, to become subjects rather than objects of their own destinies. Thus, throughout the film, the inmates are far more than mere background scenery for the conflict between McMurphy and Nurse Ratched. They become the very stakes for which the conflict is being carried out.

The way McMurphy accomplishes this liberation of the patients is worth reflecting on. He never accepts their designation as "crazy," but instead treats them as flawed but fellow human beings. Even during outdoor recreational periods on the basketball court, he is convinced he can get the "Chief" to play what McMurphy calls an "old Indian game"—basketball ("It's called, uh, put the ball in the hole")—despite the fact that the "Chief" shows no signs of being able to communicate or interact socially. While Nurse Ratched looks on with her cold, steely eyes from a window overlooking the yard, McMurphy rides atop the shoulders of Bancini, a huge, lethargic patient, while showing the "Chief" how to dunk the ball.

Throughout the film, McMurphy, in effect, creates an alternate reality for the men by convincing them that their situation need not merely be put up with. In what is undoubtedly one of the most important sequences in the film, McMurphy, after losing his second bid to watch the World Series, goes over to the couch in front of the television and pretends to be watching the game. As he re-creates a play-by-play version of the game, the other patients are lured in and begin to share in the imaginary excitement. The empty television screen reflects only their inquisitive faces. As they begin to yell and scream ("Home run! Home run!"), Nurse Ratched calls for order. What is so powerful about the scene, of course, is not only the way McMurphy is able to provide imaginary therapy for the inmates, but the reaction of Nurse Ratched, who is clearly powerless to restrain them. She may be able to control the inmates' television, but she cannot control their spirits if they refuse to let her.

When McMurphy discovers that most of the patients are voluntary and self-committed, he is amazed and bewildered. He sees them not as insane, but as victims of their own passive acceptance of life within institutional walls. He tells the inmates that they should think of themselves as no different than the nurse or the wardens, "What do you think you are, for Christ's sake, crazy or something? Well, you're not! You're not!"

In another scene, McMurphy hijacks the hospital's field trip bus, loaded with his fellow inmates. He then swings by and picks up his girlfriend, Candy, and takes them all deep-sea fishing. On board the bus, Candy turns around and asks the men, "You all crazy?" Cheswick smiles and nods affirmingly. But McMurphy does not treat them as though they are crazy. As they prepare to commandeer the charter boat, the harbor manager attempts to stop them. In a memorable scene, McMurphy informs him that the men are a group of doctors from the state mental institution. The sense of pride and seriousness with which the men accept their new identities is both hilarious and inspiring. He introduces each one of them: "This is Dr. Cheswick, Dr. Taber, Dr. Frederickson, Dr. Scanlon, the famous Dr. Scanlon, Mr. Harding, Dr. Bibbit, Dr. Martini, and Dr. Sefelt…Oh, I'm Dr. McMurphy, R. P. McMurphy." (Note, however, that Harding, who deems himself the sanest of the group, is referred to as "Mr. Harding" rather than "Dr. Harding.")

McMurphy's solidarity with the men is central to his function as Christ-figure. Like Jesus of Nazareth, the Christ-figure gathers a following from among those who are despised and cast aside. It is this motley group of society's rejects who inherit and will carry on his mission. In the same way, the message of the cross is perceived as "good news," not for the powerful and the arrogant, "those who are 'at home' in the world as it is, but for those who find themselves socially, religiously, and politically marginalized."[13] Out on the ocean, as they prepare their bait and fishing tackle, McMurphy shouts triumphantly to Martini, "You're not an idiot. Huh! You're not a…looney now, boy. You're a fisherman!" And while it may not be the author's intention, viewers who find in McMurphy the presence of a Christ-figure can't help but see the parallel here to Christ's call to his first disciples, "Follow me, and I will make you fishers of people!" The inmates come back with a large catch of fish and smiles, beaming ear to ear as they are met dockside by the police and the hospital administrator. McMurphy's defiance of the powers that be turns out to be a far more liberating form of therapy than any treatment they have received at the hospital.

Though McMurphy has a liberating impact on all the men, especially Billy, the central features of his role as a Christ-figure come into full relief against the background of his relationship with "Chief" Bromden, in whom the story finds its dramatic conclusion. During one of the group therapy sessions, when Cheswick throws a wild tantrum because Nurse Ratched refuses him access to his cigarettes, McMurphy smashes the glass panels of the nurses' station and grabs a carton of cigarettes to calm Cheswick down. One of the guards tries to restrain McMurphy and a fight ensues. McMurphy has gradually been drawing "Chief" Bromden out of his shell on the basketball court, and now the "Chief" enters the fight to help even the odds. As punishment, Cheswick, McMurphy, and "Chief" Bromden are all sent upstairs to the "disturbed" ward, where they will be subdued by electroshock treatment. As McMurphy and the "Chief" sit outside in the hall awaiting their fate, McMurphy discovers that the "Chief" is neither deaf nor mute and has been faking it all along. A relationship is struck up as McMurphy and the Chief contemplate an escape to Canada.

The electroshock treatment is the beginning of what may be interpreted theologically as "the passion of McMurphy." There is a compelling quality to McMurphy's innocent suffering as he is strapped to the bed and the electric conductors placed on his head— a "crown of thorns," so to speak. He survives the shock treatment and rejoins the group as upbeat as ever. After Billy's death and McMurphy's attack on Nurse Ratched, however, he is led away to be lobotomized, a once common procedure in mental hospitals, performed on severely disturbed patients to subdue and control them by reducing them to a totally passive and obedient state. In the context of the film, lobotomy is the perfect symbol of crucifixion. It is the ultimate instrument of the forces against which McMurphy has rebelled, much as the cross was, in Jesus' day, the ultimate punishment for those who were branded as rebels against the authority of the state.

With McMurphy's absence, rumors begin to circulate among the inmates that he has escaped. Harding, however, has learned that McMurphy has actually been taken upstairs and is, as he puts it, "as meek as a lamb." That evening as the men lie asleep, McMurphy is returned to the ward—limp as a rag doll, glassy-eyed, and unresponsive. In the film's dramatic conclusion, the "Chief" comes to McMurphy's bedside, happy his friend has rejoined him. Empowered by McMurphy, a spark has been lit in the "Chief's" soul, and he now feels "as big as a damn mountain." And then, realizing what has happened, he holds McMurphy in his arms and hugs him in a pose reminiscent of the "Pietà."[14] The "Chief" then smothers him with a pillow, refusing to leave McMurphy in such a state. Then, with the strength of two men, the "Chief" rips out the marble sink and throws it through the window, smashing the bars that keep the men imprisoned. Energized by McMurphy's life and transformed by his suffering and death, the "Chief" escapes from the cuckoo's nest. As the Chief is cheered on by shouts of victory from the other inmates, the camera follows him out into the twilight.

"Died, and was Buried. He Descended to the Dead."

The Apostles' Creed accompanies its assertion that Jesus was crucified with a reference to his death and burial and with the controversial phrase "he descended to the dead." In older translations, the latter phrase sometimes appears as "he descended into hell." The original reference, however, is to the Hebrew notion of *sheol* or *hades*, which indicated the place where dead people go—a shadowy underworld disconnected from and forgotten by the living and cut off from the power and activity of God (Ps. 88:12; Isa. 38:18). The creed here is fully affirming Jesus' death—he does not merely "pass out" on the cross, nor can we say that, as the Son of God, he could not really have died. Rather, the Christian faith affirms that Jesus partakes fully in the radical negation of human hope and future that is death.

At the same time, the creed is affirming more than merely the fact that Jesus really did die. The descent of Jesus to the dead is originally drawn from two passages in 1 Peter. In the first, Jesus is said to have been "put to death in the flesh" so that we may be "made alive in the spirit" (3:18–20). The passage goes on to claim that Jesus "went and made proclamation to the spirits now in prison." This cryptic reference is developed further in the passage that follows it: "but they shall give account to Him who is ready to judge the living and the dead. For the gospel has for this purpose been preached even to those who are dead, that though they are judged in the flesh as men, they may live in the spirit according to the will of God" (4:5–6).

These passages are by far some of the more difficult in the entire Bible to interpret, but we may at least conclude from them that all who have ever lived are included in the liberating power of Christ's death. The gospel has broken into even the realm of the dead. There is no rival power—not Satan, not demons, not the power of any domination system—that we must fear or with which we should be preoccupied. The victory is Christ's, and this victory excludes no one. Perhaps this is why, in Matthew's gospel, Jesus' crucifixion occasioned reports that "tombs were opened; and many bodies of the saints who had fallen asleep were raised; and coming out of the tombs after His resurrection they entered the holy city and appeared to many" (27:52–53). Already in the crucifixion, the sting of death is judged, and the victory of the grave is exposed as false.

QUESTIONS FOR DISCUSSION

1. How do you see the relationship between McMurphy and Nurse Ratched? What is really going on between the two of them in this film?
2. Are there ways in which you can see McMurphy as a "Christ-figure"? Are there other "religious" dimensions or allegories in this film?
3. Are there important lessons to be drawn from McMurphy's relationships with any of the other inmates?
4. How is it that Jesus' death on the cross somehow achieves our own liberation and salvation today?

RELATED FILMS

Braveheart (1995)
Breaking the Waves (1996)
Cool Hand Luke (1967)

Dead Poets Society (1989)
Edward Scissorhands (1990)
The Elephant Man (1980)
Limelight (1952)
The Passion of Joan of Arc (1928)
On the Waterfront (1954)
La Strada (1954)

NOTES

[1]Baugh, *Imaging the Divine*, 59.

[2]Baugh points out two such examples: *Raging Bull* (1980) when boxer Jake LaMotta (played by Robert DeNiro) leans back against the boxing ropes in a crucifixion pose, and *Giant* (1956) when Jett Rink (played by James Dean) stands with his head bowed and his arms resting on a rifle braced over his shoulders while Leslie Benedict (played by Elizabeth Taylor) kneels in front of him at "the foot of the cross," so to speak.

[3]*Naming the Powers: The Language of Power in the New Testament* (Philadelphia: Fortress Press, 1994); *Unmasking the Powers: The Invisible Forces that Determine Human Existence* (Philadelphia: Fortress Press, 1986); and *Engaging the Powers: Discernment and Resistance in a World of Domination* (Minneapolis: Fortress Press, 1992).

[4]Walter Wink, *The Powers That Be: Theology for a New Millennium* (New York: Doubleday, 1998), 39–40.

[5]Ibid., 35.

[6]Ibid., 83.

[7]George Orwell's futuristic novel *1984*, twice made into film, is another sobering example of this mechanism.

[8]Romans 3:25; Hebrews 2:17; 1 John 2:2; 1 John 4:10.

[9]Amos 5:22–24; Isaiah 1:10–17.

[10]Matthew 9:13; Hosea 6:6.

[11]Wink, *The Powers That Be*, 80.

[12]Ibid., 35.

[13]Jennings, *Loyalty to God*, 107.

[14]Baugh, 225.

"On the third day he rose again. He ascended into heaven, and is seated at the right hand of the Father."

Three Vignettes: *Phenomenon, Powder,* and *E.T. The Extra-Terrestrial*

The clause in the creed referring to Jesus' resurrection, his ascension, and the seating (also called "session") of Jesus at the right hand of the Father is uniquely situated as a transition from the past of Jesus to the present and future of Jesus. This chapter focuses primarily on the ascension and session of Jesus. More explicit attention to the resurrection is given in chapter 14, "the resurrection of the body and the life everlasting." For the Christian, what we believe about our own resurrection is always tied directly to the resurrection of Jesus. We would do well, therefore, to consider both his and our resurrections together.

It is impossible to talk about the ascension of Jesus, however, without some reference to the resurrection that precedes it. Throughout the New Testament, the ascension is depicted as the culmination of the entire upward movement of the Easter story[1] and as the climax of Jesus' resurrection transformation. In his first resurrection appearance to Mary Magdalene, Jesus says to her, "Stop clinging to me, for I have not yet ascended to the Father" (Jn. 20:17). At other points, the story of the ascension also serves as a way of concluding and even placing a limit on the resurrection appearances of Jesus. Jesus' bodily removal from the earth prevents ongoing attempts by those who would manipulate resurrection appearances to their own personal ends by indefinitely claiming that Jesus has appeared here or there (Mk. 13:21–22) or that this or that person is actually Jesus resurrected (Mk. 13:6). The ascension brings closure to the historical resurrection story and at the same time opens history to Jesus' resurrection power in a new and dynamic way.

At the same time, the ascension of Jesus stands in relationship to that which follows it, namely, the session of Jesus at the right hand of the Father. Here we discover the one phrase in the central section of the Apostles' Creed that is in the present tense: "Jesus *is seated.*" With these words the creed is affirming the paradox that the separation implied in the ascension is really a way of expressing the ongoing proximity of the resurrected Jesus through the Holy Spirit.[2] When we celebrate the ascension of Jesus, as theologian Karl Rahner says, "The ascension does not only have the connotation of departure and distance. On the contrary, it is a festival of the nearness of God."[3] In proclaiming the ascension, we do not proclaim Jesus' absence but his presence. Jesus is removed bodily from the world, but becomes even more immediate to the world as the one who intercedes on our behalf. As the apostle Paul says, "Christ Jesus is He who died, yes, rather who was raised, who is at the right hand of God, who also intercedes for us. Who shall separate us from the love of Christ?" (Rom. 8:34–35). It is therefore true that in the ascension, Jesus "is closer to us than he ever was; closer than he was during the time when he was still in the flesh, closer so long as his Spirit is in us."[4]

But how can it be that one who is absent from us can now be said to be even more present than before? How is it that bodily separation from Jesus paves the way for spiritual union with Jesus? We now turn to a trio of popular films (*E. T. The Extra-Terrestrial, Phenomenon,* and *Powder*), each of which portrays the removal of its central character to another plane of existence and, consequently, that character's ongoing presence in and inspiration of those who are left behind. None of the three films is explicitly religious, and yet they may all be viewed as secular allegories of the ascension and session of Christ. All three films have a similar structure, central character, and story line. Individually and as a trio, the films provide us with interesting dialogue partners in our reflection on what it means to say that Christ is risen, ascended, and seated at the right hand of God.

E. T. The Extra-Terrestrial (1982)

So obvious are the parallels between the life of Christ and that of E.T. that it is not surprising that E.T., the short, loveable alien who is accidentally stranded on earth, should so frequently be considered as a Christ-figure by viewers and critics.[5] E.T., for example, comes to the earth from the heavens. Though wise and powerful, he first appears to children and is accepted by them. He is hunted down by the establishment; he performs healing and miracles; he dies, is resurrected, and then ascends into the heavens as his earthling friends look upward, gazing into the sky.

Directed by Steven Spielberg, the story of E.T. is an enchanting, childhood fantasy told through the genre of suburban science fiction. E.T. is befriended by a ten-year-old boy, Elliot (played convincingly by Henry Thomas), with whom he develops a kind of internal, spiritual bond such that what happens to one happens to the other. Elliot, whose father has recently left the family, wants to try to "keep" E.T., but those plans are thwarted by the pragmatism of grown-ups, the obsession of government scientists, and the spoiled atmosphere of California. E.T.'s health begins to decline, and, after being captured by the scientists, he finally dies on a sterile operating table. Unknown to the scientists, however, E.T. has all along been trying to "phone home," and apparently E.T.'s messages have gotten through. Telepathic news of a retrieval party, along with Elliot's undying devotion, brings E.T. back to life, an event signaled to Elliot by the resurrection of a pot of flowers and the warm red glow of E.T.'s heart.

What is most interesting for the purposes of this chapter, of course, is the film's final scene, in which E.T. rejoins his crew and ascends into the sky. Before leaving, he gives final hugs and good-byes to each of the bystanders. When he comes to Elliot, however, the parting is especially poignant. E.T. reaches out and places on

Elliot's forehead the same glowing finger from which healing has emanated earlier in the film. As his final words draw their emotional cues from the Oscar-winning score by John Williams, E.T. proclaims, "I'll be right here." In this powerful scene of the heavenly visitor touching the human being (reminiscent of God's touching Adam in Michelangelo's "The Creation of Adam," in the Sistine Chapel), E.T. appears to implant within Elliot not a mere memory, but something of himself. Departure, distance, and absence are transformed into union, proximity, and presence. E.T. may be headed off to other parts of the universe, but he remains within Elliot.

Phenomenon (1996)

In *Phenomenon*, directed by Jon Turteltaub, George Malley (John Travolta) is knocked to the ground on the night of his thirty-seventh birthday by a "close encounter" with a bright bolt of light from the sky, and suddenly things begin to change. George, a humble auto mechanic, is instantly transformed into a genius whose mind works overtime with an insatiable thirst for knowledge and who can even move objects through telekinesis. George now reads two or three books a day, learns Portuguese in twenty minutes, and conducts homemade experiments with fertilizers, solar energy, and organic automobile fuel.

Phenomenon: ©Touchstone Pictures, Courtesy MoMA

From the beginning of the film, George tries to romance Lace, a divorced mom (played by Kyra Sedgwick) who is reticent about building any new love relationships. Not surprisingly, she eventually can't help herself, and the relationship begins to blossom. The local residents increasingly ostracize George as they become suspicious of him and a little fearful of his unexplained new powers. George's best friends, Doc (Robert Duvall) and Nate (Forest Whitaker), stand by him.

Like E. T., George is taken captive by the government and submitted to a battery of tests. He is finally released, though constantly kept under surveillance. Eventually the doctors discover that George did not, in fact, have an extraterrestrial encounter but instead suffers from a rare and inoperable brain tumor. Though the tumor allows George to use more of his brain than the average human, it is quickly killing him at the same time. As in the case of E. T., the scientists and doctors conspire with the government to dissect his brain and study it, but George escapes in order to spend his last hours peacefully with Lace and her children.

Throughout the film, we discover that what has been happening to George is that he has become more in tune with the world around him, more perceptive, and more in harmony with the forces of nature. He can even feel the vibrations of an earthquake well before it occurs. Able to make a pencil move by merely stretching out his hand toward it, he describes his ability not as some miraculous power, but as "a partnership," "a collaboration," and "a dance" between himself and the pencil. George realizes that "we're all made of the same stuff…living energy" and that we are all interconnected. In fact, George sees himself as "the possibility" of what humans may someday become if our minds were used to a fuller capacity and allowed to work *with* rather than merely *on* nature.

Critics and reviewers of *Phenomenon* have often noted its similarities to the teachings of Scientology, a quasi-religious organization (often viewed as a cult, though with the tax status of a church) founded by science fiction writer L. Ron Hubbard and of which John Travolta is himself a member. Scientologists, for example, teach that humans are, at the core of their being, immortal "thetans" (having traveled here from other parts of the universe) who, if properly trained, can harness the powers of their minds and rid themselves of pain, disease, and suffering. Through a course of study called "dianetics," Scientology attempts to teach people how to interact more fruitfully with their environments by "clearing" themselves of unwanted, unconscious memories. As Hubbard wrote, "We seek only evolution to higher states of being for the individual and for Society."[6]

It is difficult to believe that the resemblance between *Phenomenon* and Scientology is merely coincidental, but there is still much in the film that does not require a Scientology connection and that is compatible with the holistic vision of *shalom* found in the Bible. As we saw in chapter 2, *shalom* refers to a vision of humans flourishing on our planet within a harmonious and just set of relations between all living beings in God's presence. The interconnectedness of all life on the planet is hardly an insight that human beings first picked up from Scientology! Indeed, the biblical notion of *shalom* is far more holistic than Scientology's essentially dualistic relationship between soul and body and overemphasis on the human mind as the location of the soul.

Returning to our consideration of Christ's ascension and session, however, *Phenomenon* provides a remarkable allegory set up by George's own interpretation of his death, especially his final talk with Lace's two children, who are partly sad and partly angry about the fact that George is dying. George offers to them a parable of what is happening to him:

> You know, if we were to put this apple down and leave it, it would be spoiled and gone within a few days; but, if we were to take a bite of it like this, it would become a part of us and we could take it with us forever…Everything is on its way to somewhere. Everything.

Again, it is probably possible to interpret George's analysis as little more than warmed-over Scientology, but his words are actually not that far removed from the apostle Paul's own interpretation of death:

> That which you sow does not come to life unless it dies; and that which you sow, you do not sow the body which is to be, but a bare grain, perhaps of wheat or of something else…So also is the resurrection of the dead. It is sown a perishable body, it is raised an imperishable body; it is sown in dishonor, it is raised in glory; it is sown in weakness, it is

raised in power; it is sown a natural body, it is raised a spiritual body. (1 Cor. 15:36–44)

Jesus also speaks of death in a similar way: "Truly, truly, I say to you, unless a grain of wheat falls into the earth and dies, it remains by itself alone; but if it dies, it bears much fruit" (Jn. 12:24).

George's death can be interpreted as an allegory of resurrection, ascension, and session insofar as his physical death and absence is translated into a spiritual rebirth and ongoing presence. George is removed bodily but is present to Lace in her experience of the wind gently rocking the trees. George is no longer around to jot down ideas and try out experiments, but he is resurrected in the notebooks full of ideas and projects he leaves behind and in the inspiration he has given to his friends. As the film closes with Eric Clapton's "Change the World" in the background, Nate and Ella, the Portuguese woman George helped to match him up with, are bringing bushels of corn into the tavern that George used to frequent. A party has been convened to celebrate George's life on the anniversary of his birthday. Adding to the symbolism of the moment, Ella is pregnant, and we also remember that the corn brought by Nate was George's idea and was grown with George's fertilizer recipe. Though George is gone, he is nonetheless present in the dreams, memories, plans, and relationships he has inspired and continues to inspire.

Powder (1995)

Phenomenon and *Powder* were released within a year of each other, and the similarities between the two films are striking. In *Powder*, Jeremy Reid (played by Sean Patrick Flanery) is struck by a bright light from the sky, much like George Malley. In Jeremy's case, however, he has yet to be born, and the light is actually a bolt of lightning. Though his mother is killed in the accident, Jeremy survives but is born albino, hairless, and, as with George, possessed of amazing powers—both physical and mental. As with George in *Phenomenon*, Jeremy ("Powder" as he is called) is ostracized because of his abnormalities.[7] In fact, this treatment begins at birth when his father first sees him and says, "That's not my son!" Abandoned by his father, Powder is eventually discovered as a teenager in his grandparents' basement, where he has been raised. When the last of his grandparents passes away, Jeremy becomes a ward of the state in the care of counselor Jessie Caldwell (Mary Steenburgen). Until now his only contact with the outside world has been his grandparents and the books in their basement.

Like George Malley, Jeremy has telekinetic powers, a genius IQ, a photographic memory, and a symbiotic relationship with nature—especially lightning and electricity. Jeremy can feel thunderstorms approaching, and when lightning shows up he feels it wanting to come to him. After being tested, Jeremy is informed that he is "the most advanced intellect in the history of humankind." He can even hear the thoughts of others "from the inside," which naturally makes him both frightening and useful. On the one hand, he can make redneck Deputy Duncan experience firsthand the agony and fear of the deer he just shot, which he does by placing one hand on the deer while it is still lying on the ground kicking and the other hand on the deputy. The experience is enough to make Duncan get rid of every gun he owns and give up hunting altogether. On the other hand, Powder helps Sheriff Barnum (Lance Henriksen) hear the final unspoken words of his wife, who is dying of cancer, as she silently pleads for him to reconcile with their son so she can die in peace.

Like E.T., Powder is hunted down by those who misunderstand him or fear him, and more than a half-dozen times we hear him declare that he wants to "go home." While *Phenomenon* has no malevolent villains (they are merely scared of George), *Powder* features plenty of stereotypical Texas rednecks who, for some strange reason, seem to delight in persecuting him. At one point, the local group of teenage thugs strip him down and mock him, throwing him into a mud puddle. As a thunderstorm looms overhead, however, a surge of energy explodes through Powder, sending the boys sprawling and killing the chief bully. As Powder places his hands on the dead boy, he becomes a human defibrillator, and the healing electric current flowing through his fingertips brings the young man back to life again.

As with *Phenomenon*, *Powder* holds out its main character as the potential for future humanity. The local high school science teacher, Donald Ripley (Jeff Goldblum), says to Powder, "You are not just different…you have a mind that we want to evolve to." He cites Einstein as believing in life after death because "energy can never cease to exist…it relays and transforms but doesn't stop, ever." Einstein thought that if we could ever get to the point where we were using our entire brain, says Ripley, "we'd be pure energy and we wouldn't even need bodies."

The final scene in *Powder* is one of the most potentially powerful allegories of the ascension on film. Powder returns home only to find it empty. Donald Ripley and Jessie Caldwell show up, as do Duncan and Sheriff Barnum. Meanwhile, a huge thunderstorm is developing overhead, and Powder decides to take an even more radical step "toward home," so to speak. As Powder begins to walk out into the open field adjacent to his house, exposed to the storm, what will happen to him next has already been anticipated by his conversation with Missy, a young girl with whom he has begun to develop a close relationship. He has told her that inside most people is a feeling of being separated from everything when, in reality, we are not. We are, instead, "a part of absolutely everyone and everything." If we could just get beyond the obstacles in our mind whereby we are taught to be disconnected from everything, we could then begin to relate intimately and honestly to each other without hiding, lying, deception, or sarcasm.

As Powder now begins to walk toward the open field, he turns and tells Sheriff Barnum that his wife, upon her death, did not "go someplace." Instead, he says, "I felt her go, not away, just out, everywhere." Ripley again quotes Einstein, "It has become appallingly clear that our technology has surpassed our humanity." He continues, "I look at you and I think that someday our humanity might actually surpass our technology." At that, Powder begins to run through the open field and the others fall in behind, trying to stop him. As he runs with arms outstretched, lightning strikes him, and in a matter of seconds he is transformed into pure energy, vanishing with an explosion that emanates a wave of energy that passes through their bodies. The energy, of course, is Powder himself. Gasping, laughing, sensing him everywhere, they bask in his presence and gaze upward to the sky.

Commission and Intercession

All three films feature a central character who is shunned, hunted, or misunderstood because he is different and therefore frightening. All three films employ the "government is bad" convention to heighten the "official" distrust of the character and build our sympathy as viewers for him. The character nonetheless draws together those who believe in him and who come to understand that his powers, though suprahuman, are something we can all learn from and perhaps even access ourselves. Finally, the protagonist, though he must depart, leaves something of himself behind—not a relic to be idolized or an object to be venerated, but his own personal essence. It is in this sense that the protagonist "ascends," quite literally in the case of *E.T.* and *Powder,* but also in *Phenomenon.* Despite the bodily removal of the character, there is continuity between him and those who are left behind—a continuity that is both internal and intangible, yet also embodied.

So it is with the ascension and session of Jesus Christ. Words like "raised," "ascended," and "exalted" are words that point up toward the heavens. But we miss the full meaning of the ascension if we stand around gazing upward with our heads in the clouds as passive observers. On the contrary, the New Testament always associates the ascension with our commissioning by Jesus and our being entrusted with his message and ministry.[8] In the ascension, we are sent out. We inherit Christ's mission and are to embody it corporately as the church. Far from being a distancing of Jesus, the ascension is an affirmation of Jesus' ongoing ministry through the church "into all the world" (Mk. 16:15), "to all the nations" (Lk. 24:47), and "even to the remotest part of the earth" (Acts 1:8).

In addition, when the Apostles' Creed affirms that Jesus is "seated at the right hand of the Father," this is not to be construed as inactivity on Jesus' part. That Jesus is "seated at the right hand of the Father" is a phrase that appears several times in the New Testament[9] signifying not only authority ("sitting" was the posture of authority in the biblical world[10]), but the authority to liberate and save (indicated by the phrase "right hand"[11]). To say that Jesus is ascended and seated at the right hand of God is to affirm that we are commissioned by Jesus to continue his ministry throughout the world and, at the same time, that we receive ongoing power to do so. The ascension and session of Jesus, then, are not mere "add-on" events in the Christian proclamation of the gospel. They are central to the redemptive mystery that is retold through the entire chain of events, including Jesus' suffering, death, resurrection, ascension, session, and ultimately even the gift of the Holy Spirit at Pentecost.[12]

QUESTIONS FOR DISCUSSION

1. Reflect on the film you have watched. Are there elements of religious symbolism or parallels with the life of Jesus?
2. The Apostles' Creed speaks of Christ's ascension into heaven. Do you see any allegory in the film to Christ's ascension? How does the film portray the removal of the central character while still asserting his ongoing presence?
3. What do you think is at stake in the creed's claim that Jesus "is seated at the right hand of the Father"?

NOTES

[1]Jennings, *Loyalty to God*, 144.

[2]Karl Rahner, *The Content of Faith: The Best of Karl Rahner's Theological Writings* (New York: Crossroad, 1992), 330.

[3]Ibid., 329.

[4]Ibid., 330.

[5]Cf. Baugh, *Imaging the Divine*, 205; Peter Malone, "*Edward Scissorhands*: Christology from a Suburban Fairy-Tale," in *Explorations in Theology and Film*, ed. Clive Marsh and Gaye Ortiz (Oxford, U.K.: Blackwell, 1997), 81; and Gaye Ortiz, "Jesus at the Movies: Cinematic Representations of the Christ-Figure," *The Month* (December 1994): 494.

[6]L. Ron Hubbard, *Scientology: The Fundamentals of Thought* (Los Angeles: Bridge Publications, 1989), 120.

[7]The initial release of *Powder* was surrounded by controversy because its director, Victor Salva, had just served sixteen months in prison for molestation of an eleven-year-old boy who had been on the set of a previous film. *Powder* was boycotted by many for that reason, and there are a number of places in the film where one may understand Salva to be projecting himself as the one who is misunderstood and persecuted. In addition, there is one scene where the central character enjoys the physical touch of an older man and a second scene where he appears to be attracted by the sight of another boy washing up in the high school locker room.

[8]Jennings, 146; cf. Acts 1:8; Luke 24:47–48; Mark 16:15.

[9]Matthew 26:64; Mark 16:19; Romans 8:34; Colossians 3:1; Ephesians 1:20–21; Hebrews 1:3; 1 Peter 3:22.

[10]Jennings, 153.

[11]Exodus 15:1–18; Psalm 118:15–16; Matthew 25:33.

[12]Dermot Lane, *Christ at the Centre: Selected Issues in Christology* (New York: Paulist Press, 1991), 104–6.

"Will come again to judge the living and the dead"

 Flatliners

"Everything matters, everything we do matters."

Thus says Nelson Wright (Kiefer Sutherland), one of five medical students who in the film *Flatliners* (1990) take turns artificially killing and resuscitating each other in order to explore the boundaries of life and death. Fascinated by the near-death experiences of some of their patients and partially in search of fame and glory, the students decide to move beyond secondhand accounts and engage in their own direct inquiry of the subject. "Philosophy failed. Religion failed. Now it's time for medical science to try," says Nelson, the originator of the idea and the first in the group to go "flatline" (a term referring to the straight line on an electroencephalogram, or EEG, that indicates clinical death).

One after another, each of the other students follows in due course—first Joe (William Baldwin), then David (Kevin Bacon), and finally Rachel (Julia Roberts). Randy Steckle (Oliver Platt) is too cowardly to go flatline and instead provides comic relief throughout much of the film. He busies himself with narrating a running video- and audio-tape of the unfolding events for the sake of posterity and perhaps a Nobel Prize. The students become "tragically competitive," as Steckle puts it, vying with each other over who can stay dead the longest. They soon find out, however, that eternity is not at all benign, as they bring back their own personal demons and guilt trips.

Accounts of near-death experiences are well known today, as books on the subject and televised interviews with those who have experienced life after death become increasingly commonplace. Most of us have heard by now the stories of those who saw bright lights at the end of a tunnel or looked down serenely at their own bodies while attempts were being made to revive them. Written by Peter Filardi, *Flatliners* was inspired by the near-death experience of one of his own friends while on the operating table. *Flatliners*, however, departs from these more blissful accounts in favor of something more ambiguous and even frightening. Director Joel Schumacher adds to the element of horror by filming on an impressive neo-Gothic set designed to represent a university teaching hospital that looks more like an eerie cathedral complete with gargoyles, broken statues of the gods, and stained-glass windows. The film is almost always shot at night, in shadows, or in twilight halftones, calling to mind some of the great old horror movies of the past like *Franken-stein* and *Dracula*.

Flatliners: © Columbia Pictures Industries, Inc., Courtesy MoMA

Things go wrong from the very beginning in *Flatliners*. Nelson's return to life brings along with him Billy Mahone, a boy he used to pick on as a kid and whose death he accidentally caused. Billy is visible only to Nelson, but the vengeance he takes on Nelson is real and leaves scars that are visible. Nelson reports to his friends only the positive elements of his afterlife experience, never letting on that anything is wrong. The next to go is Joe, a womanizer who has been secretly videotaping his conquests. His resuscitation produces the residual effect of causing him to see hallucinatory images of the women he has slept with. Everywhere he looks the women appear to him, using the same shallow and demeaning pick-up lines he has used on them. Apparently, says *Flatliners*, what goes around comes around.

David Labraccio, the professed atheist in the group, insists on going next. Labraccio suggests that Nelson and Joe had postmortem experiences because they wanted to. As an atheist and a skeptic, he considers himself the "control" in the experiment, the one who won't see what isn't out there. Upon return to consciousness, however, Labraccio reports, "I had this feeling that if I had gone any further, there was something out there, protecting me. Something good." Labraccio also brings back some baggage, however, as he finds himself taunted by images of a young girl he used to ridicule in grade school.

Finally, Rachel gets her turn to go flatline. She has been anxious to go because one of her patients, an elderly woman, has been close to death. Rachel has recently heard joyful stories of afterlife experiences and has been assuring her patient that death is not to be feared but embraced as something beautiful. After Rachel's trip to the other side, however, she has haunting visions of her father, a war veteran, who was unable to cope with his return home. Twenty years ago, as a child, Rachel had walked in on him shooting up heroin in the bathroom. Filled with remorse, her father had shot himself, and Rachel has apparently blamed herself ever since. Now it seems her father is back. As Rachel says, "Death is beautiful? What a bunch of crap!"

As the students each go about trying to reconcile themselves with their pasts by repenting for unforgiven sins and resolving unsettled guilt, *Flatliners* employs considerable religious imagery and symbolism. The film offers explicit messages about sin, guilt, afterlife, and reconciliation that have caused some reviewers to describe it as "unbearably preachy"[1] and "heavy-handed."[2] Yet the rich cinematography and unique story line have a way of drawing viewers in and forcing them to contemplate in more than a passing way the meaning of life and the seriousness of all their actions. As with *Contact* (chapter 1), questions of religious faith surface precisely at the point where science and technology reach their limits. The film raises questions about how far one may go before trespassing on God's turf. In fact, figuring prominently in the film at its conclusion is a huge portrait of Prometheus caught in the act of stealing fire, a warning against "playing God."

Karmic Justice or Christian Judgment?

At one point in *Flatliners*, David Labraccio, the atheist, decides he will conduct his own personal quest to make peace with his past by looking up the student he once ridiculed, visiting her, and asking for forgiveness. He does, his visions disappear, and all is well. In an interesting line of dialogue, after Labraccio has made his peace, Nelson (who is still being beaten up on a regular basis by Billy) proclaims sarcastically to the others in the group, "Young Dr. Dave thinks he's solved our karmic problems: 'atonement,' gentlemen!" The interesting juxtaposition of the words "karmic" and "atonement"—words typically belonging to two very different faith traditions—prompts a number of questions for theological reflection on this film. What, for example, is the understanding of afterlife and judgment implied by *Flatliners,* and how, if at all, does that understanding compare and contrast with a Christian understanding?

In two of the world's major religious traditions, Hinduism and Buddhism, as well as a number of contemporary spiritualities that draw on those traditions, our lives and actions are subject to a moral law of cause and effect known as "karma." Karma is a permanent feature of reality, an impersonal cycle whereby all our actions, whether good or bad, create effects that determine our future. Good deeds are inevitably rewarded, and evil deeds are inevitably punished. Of course, words like "reward" and "punish" do not exactly fit a proper understanding of karma, for they imply the existence of a supreme personal being or deity who is dispensing these rewards and punishments. In a karmic view of reality, on the contrary, the consequences of evil and good are built into the universe as constant principles. We might compare the whole thing to spitting into the wind. Surely we would not claim we were "punished" by the wind. It would be more correct to say that our actions are charged positively or negatively and that these charges attach themselves to our very being, shaping who we are and the course of our lives. Indeed, almost every aspect of our lives is determined by karma—our intelligence, longevity, social status, and even our very life species.

Of course, many persons who don't believe in karma also believe that "we reap what we sow," but the doctrine of karma is much more rigorous. One's entire destiny (and future reincarnation) is dependent on the iron law of karma, so that all we do in this lifetime has eternal repercussions. Versions of Buddhism and Hinduism differ on whether we should attempt to alter karmic destiny by amassing good karma throughout our lives or whether we should instead seek liberation from rebirth and from the entire karmic cycle by following various steps to enlightenment.

There is much about the doctrine of karma that might commend itself to us. It is a doctrine of human action that appears to be exceptionally just. Every action has a corresponding and proportionate consequence. We get what we deserve. So, for example, in *Flatliners*, Joe treats women as sexual objects, pretending to love them when they are really mere conquests to him. In turn, he himself is inevitably treated as an object, eventually losing the one who loves him the most. So also, David is taunted by the girl he once taunted. Nelson is tormented by the one he once tormented. Every action has a consequence, and the interesting premise of *Flatliners*— however adequately or inadequately the film actually develops that premise—is that our futures, even beyond death, are somehow shaped by the consequences of our actions.

Christianity also holds that our choices matter eternally, and it is this to which the Apostles' Creed testifies with the phrase, "he will come again to judge the living and the dead." There are, however, at least four primary differences between a Christian understanding of human action and a karmic understanding:

1. We are judged by Jesus. For Christian faith, our lives are not subject to an impersonal law of cause and effect, nor are we measured by an abstract set of regulations or a timeless code of conduct. We are instead judged by a person, Jesus, the one who was born in a manger, had dinner with tax collectors, associated with prostitutes, and announced joy and deliverance for the poor, the weak, and the marginalized. The notion of our lives being judged is not unique to Christianity, but the notion that there is no judge other than Jesus[3] is unique—even radical—and gives a clear reference for evaluating our actions. It is by taking up the cause of Jesus and by sharing in his mission and ministry that our lives and our actions become something holy, positive, and good.

Perhaps nowhere does the Christian understanding of judgment come into full relief as clearly as in the parable of the last judgment in Matthew 25:

> But when the Son of Man comes in His glory, and all the angels with Him, then He will sit on His glorious throne. And all the nations will be gathered before Him; and He will separate them from one another, as the shepherd separates the sheep from the goats; and He will put the sheep on His right, and the goats on the left. (31–33)

Not only is Jesus the judge in this parable, but both individuals and nations are accountable before him. This notion that we are corporately responsible for the actions of our nations is a theme that runs especially throughout the Hebrew scriptures, where there is little thought given to personal judgment,[4] but it also appears here in the New Testament. The real shocker in the parable, however, is the set of criteria by which Christ makes his judgment.

> Then the King will say to those on His right, "Come, you who are blessed of My Father, inherit the kingdom prepared for you from the foundation of the world. For I was hungry, and you gave Me something to eat; I was thirsty, and you gave Me drink; I was a stranger, and you invited Me in; naked, and you clothed Me; I was sick, and you visited Me; I was in prison, and you came to Me." (25:34–36)

The parable makes the surprising point that we have been meeting our judge all along in, as Mother Teresa used to say, "the distressing disguise of the poor." In other words, what we refer to as a "final judgment" to take place in the future is really a judgment that has been occurring every day. Within this parable, interestingly enough, both the sheep and the goats are surprised to discover the significance of their previous actions. The sheep are as surprised as the goats to find out that they are actually caring for Jesus when they care for the hungry, thirsty, naked, sick, and imprisoned. Both the sheep and the goats have been taught to place priority on other more religious gauges of measuring one's goodness. Jesus, however, uses the simple gauge of whether we treat each other—and particularly the poor, outcast, sick, and imprisoned—as fellow humans. Such simplicity is revolutionary in its capacity for turning our normal ways of valuing and "judging" upside down.

2. Judgment is deliverance. In the biblical understanding, a judge is not one who tries cases and then sits back dispensing rewards and punishments. To judge is to *save* and *deliver*.[5] The judge is the one who rescues the weak and the helpless from the cruelty of the powerful and the neglect of the arrogant. The words *judgment* and *judge* have a terribly negative connotation in our contemporary culture, but in the context of the Bible they do not evoke horror, but hope. Of course, in defending the poor against the rich and in rescuing the powerless from the powerful, the judge does come into conflict with some groups over against others. The Christian notion of judgment *does* have some bite to it! But we misunderstand the nature of Christ as our judge if we think of him as a remote lawgiver who keeps scrupulous record of all our actions and thoughts and who stands ready to bring about a full reckoning some day. We might do better to translate our phrase from the Apostles' Creed, "He will come again to *deliver* the living and the dead."

3. Judgment springs from mercy. However proportionate the consequences may be to the original actions that produced them in the case of the medical students in *Flatliners*, there still appears to be something essentially unfair about those consequences. Labraccio, for example, was a mere child in grade school. Is it right that his future should be determined by the karmic baggage of those actions? Or, for example, in the case of Rachel, is she not more a victim than a culprit in her father's death? So too, though Nelson was, of course, responsible for the death of little Billy Mahone, he was a child when it occurred. As Nelson himself says while kneeling beside Billy's grave: "I was taken away from my family when I was nine years old. I was sent to Stoneham School for Boys. I thought I'd paid my dues. It was an accident!" Labraccio likewise objects as Nelson expires on the operating table: "He was just a kid! It was just a mistake. He doesn't deserve to die."

Christianity offers the protest that a karmic understanding of reality is not really all that fair and just after all. Can karma adjust for intentions and context? Can karma make any allowance for repentance and forgiveness? For Christian faith, justice is framed within a personal and covenantal relationship rather than a legal and impersonal one. And here is the subversive message of Christian faith: In Jesus of Nazareth, God gives us what we don't deserve! Indeed, the essence of Christian salvation is that we have been forgiven. Christian judgment, then, has little interest in abstract definitions of justice. According to the Apostles' Creed, the one who judges us is one who knows us and loves us, namely, Jesus of Nazareth. Justice is not some impersonal moral law of cause and effect, but a loving and merciful establishment of a new and creative justice.

Jesus' parable of the prodigal son is an excellent example at this point. When one of two sons asks his father for his half the inheritance and then squanders it in "loose living" (Lk. 15:13), he is filled with regret. He decides to return home, confess his sin, and ask to be taken back as a hired hand. In a karmic framework, the son would have to pay for his actions until the karmic effects have been worked off. In the Christian vision, on the other hand, the boy returns home, and his father accepts him with open arms. The father even prepares a feast in the boy's honor. The older brother in the story wants "justice" and "fairness." It is not right that his father should accept his brother back so freely. But in the Christian vision, justice is not an abstract or legal accounting of reward and punishment commensurate with the action. Justice begins with compassion and mercy. It is established in the context of a covenant between parent and child rather than between judge and defendant. In the end, a Christian understanding of judgment finds karma to be quite unfair and pessimistic. There is little room for grace and mercy.

4. Our choices matter because they matter to God. For Christian faith, the meaning of our lives is grounded ultimately in our contribution to the life of God and to God's reign rather than in our own personal destinies beyond the grave. Of course, most Christians believe in life after death and in heaven and hell, but what makes our choices so important is not where they will "land us" some day after we die, but whether they succeed or fail as loving responses to God's grace. In other words, it is God who ultimately matters. In the Christian vision, there is something much larger and more fundamental going on in the universe than what happens to me. Far from this vision's reducing my life to insignificance, my life and my choices have enormous significance and eternal value because they either contribute to or detract from this enormous and eternal reality, namely, God's reign.

It is for this reason that a Christian ethic is always an ethic of response rather than an ethic guided by the desire for reward and the fear of punishment. Admittedly, Christians have sometimes tended to act as if the only reason for doing good and shunning evil was to avoid hell and obtain heaven. But there is certainly nothing distinctively Christian about this narrow focus on our own immortality and our own personal destinies. Indeed, it is actually quite infantile. I can trace the same motivations in the way my dog, Schubert, avoids punishment and pursues reward. As Christians, we do not love God out of hope of reward or fear of punishment. This does not mean that my actions do not have eternal consequences for me. It is rather to stress the point that, as a Christian, what will happen to me after I die is not what brings meaning and value to my actions; rather, it is the consequences of those actions for God and God's reign.

Obviously, this starting point places the whole discussion about the consequences of human action within a different framework from that of karma. What we do matters ultimately because it matters to God and to God's reign. Our own destinies are safely held within God, and while we might speculate about the question of those destinies, the Christian first claims that our actions make a difference eternally because they make a difference to the one who is eternal.

The Future of Jesus

"He will come again to judge the living and the dead." Perhaps no statement in the creed has evoked as much speculation, distortion, or imagination. Throughout history there have been groups such as the Montanists in the second century or Jehovah's Witnesses, Seventh Day Adventists, and other conservative evangelical groups in the twentieth century who have made the second coming of Christ the center and preoccupation of Christian worship, faith, and practice. Taking what is but one in a complex of ideas that make up Christian hope, these Christians have moved beyond the simple prayer "Come, Lord Jesus" (Rev. 22:20) to interpret virtually every historical event as a sign of the last days and of Jesus' imminent arrival.

But merely because one's life is oriented toward the future does not mean that one's life is oriented in hope. To reduce faith in Christ's return to a preoccupation with "calendarizing" that event while neglecting our concrete and present participation in the reign of God can hardly be understood as hopeful. John Calvin once said, "Satan directly attacks the throat of the Church when he destroys faith in the return of Christ."[6] It is possible, however, that a distorted preoccupation with Christ's return (see, for example, the film *The Rapture*) can actually become a destruction of authentic faith. A preoccupation with Christ's return may indeed be quite pessimistic and escapist. On the other hand, to pray "Come, Lord Jesus" is to pray the prayer that Jesus himself prayed, "Thy kingdom come. Thy will be done, on earth as it is in heaven" (Mt. 6:10).

Paradoxically, the simple claim from the creed "He will come again to judge the living and the dead" combines two claims that might at first seem like opposites. "He will come again" expresses hope in the return of Christ and is a statement of our confidence that the last word does not lie within our own powers and our own agendas. "To judge the living and the dead," on the other hand, expresses a confidence in the significance of our actions and choices and affirms the tremendous responsibility that is placed in our paths each moment of each day. So on the one hand, all that we do matters. On the other hand, we ought never to rely wholly on our own actions and plans, nor ought we to make our own futures ultimate. Our hope is in the future of Jesus, and in that future we find cause for neither horror nor distraction, but for alertness and engagement.

QUESTIONS FOR DISCUSSION

1. How do you feel about the way the film portrays the post-mortem effects of our actions in this life?
2. How would you compare and contrast the Christian vision of judgment with that of other religions you know about?
3. For Christians, why do our actions matter?

4.   Is there any special significance to the Apostles' Creed's claim that it is Christ who is our judge?

RELATED FILMS

Defending Your Life (1991)
The Rapture (1991)

NOTES

[1]Pauline Kael, *5001 Nights at the Movies*, 333.
[2]Joe Brown, "Flatliners," *Washington Post*, August 10, 1990.
[3]Jennings, *Loyalty to God*, 161.
[4]Marthaler, *The Creed*, 206–7.
[5]Jennings, 162ff.
[6]Cranfield, *The Apostles' Creed*, 50.

10

"I believe in the Holy Spirit"

 ***Star Wars***

"May the Force be with you."

In 1977, *Star Wars*, directed by George Lucas, became the number one grossing film in the United States and retained that status until being unseated by *Titanic* in 1998. Its sequels, *The Empire Strikes Back* (1980) and *Return of the Jedi* (1983), also hold places in the top ten highest grossing films of all time in the United States.[1] That no film in almost a quarter century of American life could rival the popularity of this film is an amazing achievement in itself and a testimony to the profound impact of the *Star Wars* films in shaping American culture. Who does not know about Luke Skywalker, Darth Vader, or R2D2? Who has not heard the now classic benediction, "May the Force be with you"? Rarely do films enter into the collective self-understanding of a culture the way *Star Wars* has. At the time of this writing, *The Phantom Menace* (1999) has just been released and likewise shows every indication of continuing the legacy of its predecessors (which, of course, are actually its sequels).

Built into the *Star Wars* films are many of humanity's most enduring mythological themes, a fact that is signaled to us at the beginning of the film, which, though it is set in the future, begins with the words, "Long ago . . ." *Star Wars* is centrally about the struggle between good and evil in which the hero warrior must rescue the princess from the clutches of an evil warlord. That epic tale is then set within the cosmic framework of "the Force," a single, invisible, and all-inclusive energy field that shapes and controls everything, including individual destinies. Belief in and devotion to this mysterious Force especially marks a band of priest-warriors known as the "Jedi." As described by Obi-wan Kenobi, one of the Jedi masters, the Force is "an energy field created by all living things. It surrounds us. It penetrates us. It binds the galaxy together." Though the Force of *Star Wars* resembles elements of Zen philosophy and ancient Chinese Taoism, it also has characteristics that make it an interesting dialogue partner for reflecting on the Christian affirmation "I believe in the Holy Spirit."

The Holy Spirit: Universal Force or Intimate Presence?

Belief in the Holy Spirit did not originate with Christianity, but was inherited from the Jewish notion of God's Spirit, portrayed in the Hebrew Scriptures as the movement of God's "breath," "wind," or "air," which creates and sustains all life. Already in the second verse of Genesis, God's Spirit is found blowing over the surface of the waters as the agent of creation. And though Hebrew writers may at times use the metaphor of God "sending" the Spirit, the Spirit is never something detachable from God.[2] It is God's active presence and agency in the world.

On the one hand, the Spirit is a way of talking about God's universal and inescapable presence:

> Where can I go from Thy Spirit? Or where can I flee from Thy presence? If I ascend to heaven, Thou art there; if I make my bed in Sheol, behold, thou art there. If I take the wings of the dawn, if I dwell in the remotest part of the sea, even there Thy hand will lead me, and Thy right hand will lay hold of me. (Ps. 139:7–10)

It is this universality of the Spirit that, in the New Testament, becomes precisely the basis for the church's calling to be a universal, or "catholic" body (see chapter 11). As a creation of the Spirit, the church knows no boundaries. On the other hand, the Spirit is a way of talking about God's local action in particular situations and in specific human lives. In the Hebrew Scriptures, the Spirit can "come upon" a prophet, inspiring him to see visions or to speak

God's word, sometimes in a state of ecstatic frenzy. In fact, the future Messiah is portrayed as one who will be "supremely endowed" with the Spirit.[3] In the New Testament, this localized activity of the Holy Spirit is especially accentuated as a transforming, empowering, and sanctifying work in the life and ministry of the church and in the saints who together comprise the church.

Clearly, the Holy Spirit does bear some resemblance to the Force of *Star Wars*. The Holy Spirit not only is the "life-force" of the universe, but also guides the destinies of individuals and can be experienced by them. As with the Force, the Holy Spirit is both cosmic and intimate, universal and local. In contrast to the Holy Spirit, however, the Force of *Star Wars* is impersonal and in no way is meant to serve as shorthand for the activity or presence of a supreme being or deity. The Force is much more like the *Tao* (pronounced "dow"), which in Chinese thought is understood as the all-embracing, harmonious principle that holds the universe together. The word *Tao* literally means the "way" of the universe. It contains within itself the basic dualities of life (the *yin* and the *yang*): good and evil, light and dark, dry and wet, male and female. In *Star Wars*, for example, not only can the Force be used for good, it has what is referred to as a "dark side," which can seduce and finally control a person like Anakin Skywalker (who becomes Darth Vader). Indeed, in the most recent installment in the series, *The Phantom Menace*, there is considerable talk throughout the film about seeking "a balance" in the Force with the hope that young Anakin Skywalker might be the (messianic[4]) figure to accomplish this. As we already know from the first trilogy, however, Anakin does not accomplish this (it is left to his son, Luke), and instead brings both himself and the galaxy under the ever increasing power of the dark side. Notice, however, that the hope expressed in *The Phantom Menace* is not for a victory over the dark side of the Force, but the more Taoist hope for a restoration of "balance" within the Force.

A Christian, however, would have difficulty speaking of the Holy Spirit in the dualistic terms of the Force or the Tao (though there have been similarly dualistic influences on Christianity over the centuries[5]). That is not to say that the Holy Spirit fits into a neat package, always bringing with it the "good" as we humans might define "good."[6] The Holy Spirit is God's creative, mysterious power, which often defies logic and definition. Still, the Christian would be unable to talk about the "dark side" of the Holy Spirit if what is meant by that phrase (as is clearly indicated in *Star Wars*) is a dimension of evil.

Also in contrast to the Force or Tao, the Holy Spirit is not to be thought of by Christians as a strictly *impersonal* power or principle in the universe. That is primarily because we speak of God in personal terms and also because we are taught in the New Testament to identify the Holy Spirit as the Spirit of Christ.[7] It is therefore improper to refer to the Holy Spirit as an "it" or "thing." In fact, the Hebrew word for Spirit, *ruach*, is of feminine gender, lending support to the idea espoused by some theologians that the Spirit should be considered the feminine member of the Trinity and thereby justifying their use of the pronoun *she* to refer to the Holy Spirit when speaking in the third person.

The Holy Spirit and Our Spirits

Just as all creation comes into being and is sustained by the presence of God's Spirit, so it is that the Hebrew Scriptures especially understand the human spirit in relation to God's Spirit. "The Spirit of God has made me, and the breath of the Almighty gives me life...If he should gather to himself his spirit and his breath, all flesh would perish together, and [humanity] would return to dust."[8] God's Spirit is the source of human strength, wisdom, and even skills related to craftsmanship.[9] It is a surge in the divine Spirit, for example, that allows Samson to tear apart a lion and conquer an entire army with the jawbone of a donkey. As already mentioned, the Spirit's rushing in on individuals can cause them to see visions and to prophesy. The Spirit is also the source of leadership (Num. 11).

Though God's Spirit dramatically seizes an individual or endows this or that person with unique gifts and capacities, there is nonetheless the hope that someday God will pour out the Spirit on all humans. As the prophet Joel says,

> And it will come about after this that I will pour out My Spirit on all mankind; and your sons and daughters will prophesy, your old men will dream dreams, your young men

will see visions. And even on the male and female servants I
will pour out My Spirit in those days. (2:28-29)

This hope, however, is for far more than the mere inspiration of
individual human beings. The Hebrew vision of the outpouring of
the Holy Spirit is consistently bound up with a broader hope "for
the renewal of the ravaged land, of the nation, and of its relationship
to God."[10] The future hope of the Holy Spirit is a corporate hope—
one that will restore the people of Israel as "a people" and bring
about *shalom*.

It is this very hope, then, that the apostle Peter believed had
begun to be fulfilled on the day of Pentecost (Acts 2) when the
Holy Spirit came rushing in on the early Christians, filling them
with power, joy, and boldness. Peter's sermon at Pentecost even uses
the very text of Joel quoted above. A new, vibrant community called
"church" was born that day, one marked by a communal sharing of
property, a special concern for the poor, an overcoming of racial
barriers, and a public witness to and modeling of God's reign. In
the experience of the first Christians, the Holy Spirit was a dramatic
force, or power that dwelled within them (1 Cor. 3:16), made them
holy and righteous (1 Cor. 6:11), brought about unity (Eph. 4:3–4),
gifted them with unique abilities for building up the body of Christ
(Eph. 4:12), and produced "fruits" that combined a renewed inner
disposition with outward ethical behavior (Gal. 5:16–23).

Likewise, in *Star Wars*, "the Force is what gives the Jedi his power,"
and, according to Obi-wan Kenobi, "a Jedi can feel the Force flowing through him." In the original *Star Wars* trilogy, just how this is
possible is left a mystery (as it is in the Bible). We do know that
through careful discipline and training at the feet of a spiritual master the Force can be channeled by the Jedi. It therefore partially
controls the Jedi's actions and partially obeys his commands. In *The
Phantom Menace*, however, George Lucas goes a step farther and
adds the presence of microscopic particles in the bloodstream called
midiclorians. These particles are present in especially high concen-
trations in the Jedi and are apparently some sort of spiritually sensi-
tive receptors that allow a person to hear and commune with the
Force. The Force itself is no less mysterious a presence because of
this additional biological factor, but the midiclorians do tend to

reduce the human relationship with the Force to a physical set of mechanics. In fact, it is questionable whether one should really go around saying "the Force be with you," given these particles. The Force is an energy field that always surrounds us, but some of us are more able to interact with it than others, based on the concentration of midiclorians in our bloodstreams!

This fact that the Force is more powerful in some families than in others was already hinted at in the original trilogy, of course. But this new twist bolsters a spiritual elitism based on genetics that was already incipient in the *Star Wars* films. As Robert Jewett says, *Star Wars* relies on "the leadership of royalty and the martial instinct of an inspired few rather than on public, moral reflection as the keys to action."[11] Here again, though there are some similarities between the Force and the Holy Spirit, the comparison breaks down. In fulfillment of Joel's prophecy that the Spirit will be poured out on all flesh, the New Testament views the presence of the Holy Spirit as that which creates an equality and unity among us rather than an elitism based on heredity, race, status, or power. It is for that reason that Simon the Magician cannot buy the gift of the Holy Spirit from the Apostles (Acts 8:9–24). As Paul says, "To each one is given the manifestation of the Spirit for the common good" (1 Cor. 12:7).

Neither can the Holy Spirit be manipulated or commanded as with the Force of *Star Wars*. True, the Christian does engage in spiritual disciplines such as fasting, prayer, worship, works of mercy and justice, or meditation in order to become more attuned to the leading of the Spirit. The Spirit, however, is the power and presence of God among us and within us that, like the wind, "blows where it wishes" (Jn. 3:8). We commune with and are led by the Spirit not because we have microscopic spiritual antennae, but rather because we are created as spirits by a God who is also Spirit. According to the apostle Paul, "The Spirit himself bears witness with our spirit that we are children of God" (Rom. 8:16).

This fact that the Spirit blows where it wishes is a warning against our "placing God in a box" or reducing Christian life to a set of rules and regulations. Legalism is deadly, but "the Spirit gives life" (2 Cor. 3:6) and brings liberty (2 Cor. 3:17). This does not mean that the Holy Spirit is some capricious, whimsical force in the universe. Rather, the Spirit is the Spirit of Christ and does not speak independently of Christ or on the Spirit's own initiative. Neither does the Spirit offer new revelations, but rather bears witness to Jesus, bringing to remembrance what he said (Jn. 14:26; 15:26; 16:13–14). It is in this sense that we may talk of the "shyness" of the Holy Spirit—not a shyness of timidity, but of other-centeredness.[12] The Holy Spirit does not draw attention to itself, but to Christ.

Perhaps the greatest difference between the Force of *Star Wars* and the Holy Spirit of Christian faith is the relationship of each to coercive violence. The very fact that the word *Force* was chosen to describe ultimate reality already reveals the bias in *Star Wars* toward warfare and violence. The irony here, of course, is that *Star Wars* intends to portray the Force as a spiritual rather than physical quality in the cosmos. When being pulled into the Death Star by a tractor beam, Obi-wan advises, "You can't win, but there are alternatives to fighting." Likewise, Jedi master Yoda says, "The Jedi uses the Force for knowledge and defense, never for attack." And yet in every *Star Wars* episode, violence is scripted into each climactic scene and underscores the entire plot as the ultimate vehicle for redemption. The Jedi may be an enlightened group of spiritual masters who know alternatives to fighting, but *Star Wars* exercises no creativity in demonstrating their ability to rise above the same tactics their enemies employ. On the contrary, recurring throughout *Star Wars* is one of our civilization's oldest, deadliest, and most persuasive myths, the myth of redemptive violence. The ultimate victory of good over evil finally boils down to firing laser-blasters, detonating bombs, or slicing through one's enemies with a light saber.

Though the presence of God's Spirit can be said to empower someone like Samson to defeat an entire army, the "force" of the Holy Spirit is regularly contrasted to physical force or coercion throughout the Bible. As the prophet Zechariah says, "'Not by might nor by power, but by My Spirit,' says the LORD of hosts" (4:6). Likewise the psalmist records, "Some boast in chariots, and some in horses; but we will boast in the name of the LORD, our God" (20:7). This is all the more true for the Christian who understands the Holy Spirit as the Spirit of Christ. Not only did Christ instruct us not to repay evil for evil and instead to "turn the other cheek," so also Paul advises the Romans never to take revenge and to instead "overcome evil with good" (Rom. 12:17–19). Repeatedly the New Testament reminds us that life in the Spirit is a life of peace[13] and that the mind that is set on the Holy Spirit is given to both life and peace (Rom. 8:6). Not only do spirit-filled Christians seek peace, they also rely on the Spirit's own means for achieving peace— patience, kindness, gentleness, forgiveness, sacrifice, and self-giving.

To believe in the Holy Spirit, then, is to live one's life in openness to an alternate reality and to see the world with a different set of eyes. To believe in the Holy Spirit is, as Paul would say, to "walk according to the Spirit." Loyalty to this Spirit, as we shall see in the following chapters, implies a life in the community created by the Spirit so that there can be no such thing as solitary, spirit-filled Christians. Likewise, the Holy Spirit is the bond that unites all God's people throughout the world and throughout time in a "communion of saints." So it is that the phrases "I believe in the holy catholic church" (chapter 11) and "I believe in the communion of saints" (chapter 12) are not independent from, but rather an explication of, the phrase "I believe in the Holy Spirit." In the same way, the phrases "I believe in the forgiveness of sins" (chapter 13) and "I believe in the resurrection of the body and the life everlasting" (chapter 14) are internally related to our belief in the Holy Spirit. Just as the Holy Spirit bears witness to us that we are forgiven and therefore the children of God, so also the power of the Spirit creates within us the revolutionary capacity for forgiving the unforgivable. Ultimately, of course, the presence of the Holy Spirit is a down payment from God that points us in hope toward the redemption of our bodies and, indeed, toward the redemption of all creation (Rom. 8:22). May the Holy Spirit be with us! May we be available to the Holy Spirit!

QUESTIONS FOR DISCUSSION

1. What religious symbolism, if any, do you see in the *Star Wars* films?
2. With what you know of the Holy Spirit in Christianity, in what ways, if any, is it similar to the Force of *Star Wars*?
3. In what ways is it different?

NOTES

[1]In addition, all three films are in the top twenty highest grossing films internationally. All figures are taken from Exhibitor Relations Co., Inc.

[2]Alasdair I. C. Heron, *The Holy Spirit* (Philadelphia: Westminster Press, 1983), 8.

[3]Ibid., 16-17; cf. Isaiah 11 42:1 4.

[4]The film even hints at the virgin birth of Anakin.

[5]Such was the case with Manichaeism, an ancient dualistic religion with its origins in Persia and with extensive influence throughout the world during the early centuries of Christianity. Saint Augustine himself was a Manichaean for a number of years before his conversion to Christianity.

[6]In fact, in more primitive strands of the Old Testament, one can even find that God on occasion sends an "evil spirit" (Judg. 9:23; 1 Sam. 16:14; 1 Kings 22:22). The usage of the word "spirit" here reflects the more impersonal sense of one's "state of mind." So, for example, if a man becomes jealous, the Hebrew would say that a "spirit of jealousy" has come upon him. This is not unlike the way an African tribal religion might talk even today. Cf. Heron, 5–9.

[7]Romans 8:9; Philippians 1:19; 1 Peter 1:11; John 14:26; 15:26; 16:13–14.

[8]Job 33:4; 34:14–15.

[9]Exodus 35:31–35.

[10]Heron, *The Holy Spirit*, 17–20.

[11]Robert Jewett, *St. Paul at the Movies* (Louisville: Westminster/John Knox Press, 1993), 29.

[12]See Frederick Dale Bruner and William Hordern, *The Holy Spirit—Shy Member of the Trinity* (Minneapolis: Augsburg).

[13]Romans 14:17–19; 15:13; Galatians 5:22; Ephesians 4:3.

11

"The holy catholic church"

 *The Mission*

John Wesley, founder of Methodism, once said, "A more ambiguous word than this, the *Church*, is scarce to be found in the English language."[1] That ambiguity is at the heart of Roland Joffé's *The Mission* (1986), the story of Jesuit missions in South America caught in the crossfire of eighteenth-century geopolitics. Featuring Academy Award–winning cinematography, *The Mission* highlights the injustices committed against the Guarani Indians in and around the borders of Argentina, Paraguay, and Brazil by the colonial powers of Portugal and Spain. The complex and complicated role of the church amid these injustices parallels many of the dynamics of the church in Latin America in the last half of the twentieth century. Indeed, *The Mission* makes no attempt to hide the fact that it intends to offer the situation of the Guarani and the priests who sided with them as a historical lesson relevant to the struggle for liberation from oppressive powers among indigenous peoples on the same continent today. The film closes with an explicit reference to the contemporary situation that sets the entire film within this broader concern:

> The Indians of South America are still engaged in a struggle to defend their land and their culture. Many of the priests who, inspired by faith and love, continue to support the rights of the Indians for justice, do so with their lives.

The light shines in the darkness and the darkness has not overcome it.
John Chapter 1, verse 5

What makes *The Mission* both fascinating and frustrating as a film about the church is that it affords us a glimpse of so many

The Mission: © Warner Bros., Inc., Courtesy MoMA

different "faces" of the church. In the first place, the film is narrated as a letter to the pope by Cardinal Altamirano (played by Irish actor Ray McAnally), who has been sent to preside over the transition of certain portions of Spanish territory to the Portuguese, which was decided in the Treaty of Madrid in 1750. Specifically, the cardinal is present to determine the fate of the Jesuit missions that will now end up in Portuguese territory. The Jesuit missions have been present on the continent for more than a century,[2] but their future is unsure, as is their relationship to the Guarani Indians, among whom they have been ministering. The film provides a small taste of the complicated inner workings of the delicate church-state relationship in the courts of eighteenth-century Europe. The church is portrayed as a powerful institution that, while still a political force to be reckoned with, has begun to lose its grip as the center of Western civilization. This church often appears to care primarily about its own self-preservation and is preoccupied with matters of raw power and influence.

In contrast to this crass institutional face of the church, and yet in many ways overlapping with it, is a portrayal of the church as an evangelizing force that sends its missionaries to the farthest reaches of the sparsely inhabited jungles of Latin America to make converts. We discover this second image of the church primarily through the priests in the film, all of whom are members of the Society of Jesus (known as "Jesuits"). The Jesuits are a long-standing religious order within Catholicism dating back to the middle of the sixteenth century and the genius of its founder, Ignatius of Loyola. The Jesuits have typically been marked by their strictness of obedience within a military-like structure and careful attention to spiritual exercises in the service of missionary and evangelizing activity. The film opens with the martyrdom of a Jesuit priest who is strapped to a wooden cross by the Guarani and sent floating down the river and over the magnificent Iguaçu Falls. Jeremy Irons plays Father Gabriel, the intensely spiritual priest who is the head of the Jesuit missionaries and who climbs the treacherous falls to continue the work of evangelizing the Guarani. For some reason, perhaps because of his music, Father Gabriel is accepted by the Indians, and a new mission is founded.

On the one hand, this missionary face of the church is consistently portrayed in the film as noble and benevolent. The priests endure hardship and adversity in their efforts to assist the Guarani. They engage in an unwavering struggle to protect their new converts from Portuguese slave traders and from Spanish mercenaries who engage in hunting, capturing, and selling the Indians to the Portuguese, despite the illegality of slave trading under Spanish law. The priests organize the Indians into cooperative and communal farming villages. It is even said that in the original missions, the Jesuits instituted policies of no capital punishment, no currency, and no private property.[3] According to Father Daniel Berrigan, modern-day Jesuit priest, peacemaker, activist, and advisor on the film (with a cameo appearance as one of the priests):

The eighteenth-century Jesuits made in the wilderness a haven for a decimated and defeated people. A haven and more. The missions were also a splendid, embodied image of soul. Which is to say, the Jesuits created for all to see, to praise, condemn, or emulate—an image of the majestic humanism and generous variety of their own spirit."[4]

On the other hand, the missionary enterprise bears some similarities to the very colonial powers with which it came into conflict. To the extent that the church is attempting to supplant Indian culture with its own, it resembles in many ways the imperialist powers of Spain and Portugal that are attempting to do likewise.[5] The danger is always present that the evangelism and missionary activity of the church will become another form of what Brazilian educator Paulo Freire calls "cultural invasion." Indeed, as Cardinal Altamirano says in the film, "I still couldn't help wondering whether these Indians would not have preferred that the sea and wind had not brought any of us." Sometimes physical, sometimes more covert, cultural invasion strips the values and goals of a people and, as Freire says, causes the invaded to "come to see their reality with the outlook of the invaders rather than their own."[6] Too often, in the church's eagerness to share Christ and lead others to salvation, we can actually do more harm than good without great care and respect for those to whom we are ministering.[7]

Still, the film goes out of its way to distinguish the Jesuit priests, who live in simplicity and considerable solidarity with the Indians, from the institutional church with all of its trappings of power, wealth, and finery. One of these Jesuit priests, played by Robert De Niro, is Rodrigo Mendoza, a former mercenary. When Rodrigo discovers that his wife has fallen in love with his brother, he kills him. Then, filled with remorse, he locks himself away in a church, presumably to waste away his days. Father Gabriel meets Rodrigo and extends to him forgiveness. Rodrigo summarily rejects the offer, considering himself beyond hope. Father Gabriel then challenges him to perform a penance, a visible and physical embodiment of contrition and repentance. Rodrigo accepts the challenge, partially to prove to the priest that no penance is proportionate to the sin he has committed or the despair he is experiencing. A penance is devised that includes dragging his full set of armor and weapons up the falls and the steep cataract that leads to the jungles where he had previously hunted the Guarani.

The road to forgiveness through penance is one that Protestant churches have generally rejected since the Reformation of the sixteenth century with its attack on a deteriorated system that reduced salvation to a crude, mechanical transaction between the individual and the church. *The Mission*, however, offers a stirring portrayal of the capacity for penance to serve as a meaningful and authentic path to salvation—one that engages the whole person, body and soul, in turning from sin to forgiveness. Once the priests arrive at the top of the falls, with Mendoza stumbling and dragging his sins behind him, one of the Guarani approaches the exhausted and despondent mercenary, once his enemy, puts a knife to his throat, and, to all appearances, threatens to kill him. Instead of killing him, however, and in a moving depiction of conversion, he cuts loose the enormous weight that Mendoza has been carrying and lets it fall into the river below. Mendoza experiences genuine forgiveness conferred by God's church, the Guarani, those Mendoza once oppressed. Here we discover a third face of the church—neither the powerful and elaborate institution behind Cardinal Altamirano nor the strict missionary order of Father Gabriel, but a simple community of the reconciled and liberated, those who extend reconciliation and liberation to their neighbor and to their enemy.

Mendoza gives up his life of slave trading and becomes a Jesuit priest, assisting Father Gabriel and the others in creating the new mission and building the village. The day arrives, however, when Altamirano must make a decision about the future of the missions, and in the end he finds he has little choice. He orders the Jesuits to abandon the missions and to exert their influence on the Indians to prevent them from organizing armed resistance. Though the film does not depict it, history shows that some of the Jesuits obeyed, as did some of the Guarani.[8] The film version, however, culminates with a number of Jesuit priests—most notably, Mendoza and Gabriel—deciding to disobey the authority of the church and to remain with the mission.

The two priests, however, take very different paths in expressing their solidarity with the Indians. Mendoza recovers his weapons and helps organize some of the priests and Indians into a small, armed rebellion. Father Gabriel, on the other hand, rejects violence and instead celebrates a mass with the Indians during the onslaught—an act that is intensely spiritual while at the same time a political act of resistance to the powers of domination. In the final moments of the destruction both Mendoza and Gabriel are shot and killed, each within sight of the other—a powerful image that forces us to weigh their respective paths and find value in both, regardless of the path with which we might more closely identify. Father Berrigan writes, "It is to the honor of the film and its makers, that the story purposes to settle nothing. Its task is more rigorous and more modest—to raise questions, to summon the intelligence and evoke the moral capacity of its viewers."[9]

The Holy Church

It is difficult to know where to begin when speaking of the origins of the church. Perhaps we should start with Pentecost, the dramatic outpouring of the Holy Spirit following Jesus' resurrection. In this event, a small rabble of huddled Christians were driven out of an upper room in Jerusalem and into the streets and the world to proclaim Christ and his "Way" and, indeed, to model that "Way" in the form of a community given over to praise and worship, testimony and evangelism, acts of compassion, and the overcoming of racial barriers and economic inequality. Or perhaps we should look for the beginnings of the church in the small community of disciples that Jesus himself formed during his own life, though it is not entirely clear that what we now call the church is what Jesus had in mind. In the often-repeated words of Alfred Loisy, "Jesus foretold the kingdom, and it was the Church that came."[10]

The Greek word for church, *ekklesia*, literally means "those who are called out (or chosen)" and refers to an assembly or congregation of people. The word originally had a political connotation designating a group of citizens gathered together to make decisions about the affairs of their local community.[11] In the Greek translation of the Old Testament, however, the word was used to translate the Hebrew word *qahal*, "the people of God," so that when also used of the New Testament church, a vital link is established to God's long history of calling together a people. This notion of "calling" is essential to the meaning of the church so that "the Church is a *convocation* before it is a *congregation*."[12] Wherever we might wish to locate the birthday of the church, however, its origins are firmly located in God's Holy Spirit. The church is a creation of the Spirit, a calling together of diverse people not on the basis of race, gender, civic loyalties, or political preference, but on the basis of a common liberation from bondage and domination accomplished by the Spirit and a corresponding pledge of loyalty to God's reign in the world through the Spirit.

It is significant that the Apostles' Creed should begin its identification of the domain of the Holy Spirit with reference to the holy catholic church and (as we shall see in the following chapter) the communion of the saints.[13] These references give to Christian belief in the Holy Spirit an essentially corporate or social emphasis rather than the more individualistic, inward, and personal emphasis so characteristic of Western culture and the types of Christianity that have flourished in that culture.[14] The very idea that God's presence and power should be understood primarily as a communal presence and that his new creation should be understood primarily as the creation of a new community runs against the grain of our usual patterns of thinking, to say the least. The point here is not that individuals do not personally experience the Holy Spirit, nor is it the case that the Holy Spirit may not be experienced inwardly. But whatever we may mean by such experiences, the Apostles' Creed directs our attention to the public and social realities of the holy catholic church and the communion of saints as the starting point for our experience of, trust in, and loyalty to the Holy Spirit.

This starting point is especially crucial when we consider the creed's audacious claim that the church is "holy," the first of two words that modify "the church." Originally, the word *holy* meant "distinct," "set apart," or "withdrawn from ordinary use."[15] Throughout the Bible, God is referred to as holy, but so also are people, objects, buildings, or even certain days of the week and year. The Hebrew prophets reacted strongly against this purely ceremonial understanding of holiness and advocated an understanding of holiness as having to do with our moral character, our loyalty to the poor, our care for widows and orphans, and even our business dealings. Throughout the New Testament, Christians themselves are referred to as holy. Indeed, the word *saints* (which refers to all members of the church) literally means "holy ones." Both in the New Testament[16] and in the Apostles' Creed, we find that the church itself is called holy. The problem is this: The church doesn't look very holy! So wherein lies the holiness of the church? In its clergy? In the correct performance of its sacraments? In the personal and moral life of its members?

Early in the history of Christianity, the church rejected the notion that its holiness somehow lies in its clergy. In the fourth and fifth centuries, in what came to be known as "the Donatist controversy," one faction of Christians declared that the consecration of a particular bishop was invalid because it had been performed by another bishop who was deemed immoral, having lapsed under persecution. This would have meant that the holiness of the church was located in the holiness of its clergy and, by extension, that all sacraments performed by unholy clergy are null and void. Imagine finding out after your wedding that the officiating clergy had been embezzling funds from your church. Would your matrimony still be holy and valid? The church has generally argued against the view of the Donatists (though with some inconsistency), teaching instead that the church's holiness is ultimately independent of the personal holiness of its clergy and the right performance of Christian rituals (that is not to say, of course, that the church is uninterested in the personal holiness of its clergy!). The holiness of the church, on the contrary, is grounded in the holiness of the Spirit, its Creator, and in the holiness of Jesus Christ, its Head.

Along the same lines, the assertion that the church is holy does not mean that its members (either personally or collectively) are therefore sinless. Such a pretense inevitably leads those outside the church to think of Christians as hypocrites. It further leads those within the church to a stultifying attempt to regulate Christian life and to distinguish sharply between sinners and saints, thereby excluding those who do not measure up.[17] This ever-present danger of equating our own personal holiness with the holiness of the church yields perilous consequences such as hyped-up emotionalism, repressive legalism, and sacred formalism that readily surface as empty substitutes for the authentic holiness by which the church is to be marked.

Despite the fact that the holiness of the church cannot be reduced subjectively to the sinlessness of its members or objectively to its clergy, institution, and sacraments,[18] there is, nonetheless, a holiness that the church is called to reflect in its life and witness.

The church cannot merely say "we stand on Christ's holiness" without allowing the allegiances and loyalties of Christ to characterize its nature and practice. To do so is to excuse our failure to follow Christ, and to rely on what Dietrich Bonhoeffer, German theologian and martyr, called "cheap grace."

> Cheap grace is the preaching of forgiveness without requiring repentance, baptism without church discipline, communion without confession, absolution without personal confession…cheap grace is grace without discipleship, grace without the cross, grace without Jesus Christ.[19]

To speak with the Apostles' Creed of the "holy" church, then, is to speak of a radical community that models on Earth what God is up to in Jesus of Nazareth. If we return to our film, however, we can see how difficult a line this is to walk.

In *The Mission*, the Jesuit missionaries are intent on creating a visible manifestation of the holy church—an inclusive community where suffering and abuse are eliminated and the humanity of the Indians is respected. To follow Christ has concrete meaning here. There is no hiding behind the old distinction between the "visible church" and "invisible church" whereby the "real" church is said to be visible only to God and not to be confused with the physical, visible, and institutional presence of the church on earth.[20] What the Jesuits help us to understand, on the contrary, is that the church is indeed an institution. There is no way of avoiding that. The church, if it really is to be the church, must have a palpable, concrete presence and activity in the world. Thus, when it comes to being the church, "what you see is what you get." Though the church is never to be simply equated with God's reign on earth, it is called to be a sign and sacrament of that reign, to be a visible instrument of God's purpose and a live model of God's inclusive activity.

And yet how short a step it is from this to Cardinal Altamirano's response to the Indians who "don't understand why God has changed his mind" in the decision to close the missions and who now question whether the cardinal truly speaks for God. Altamirano has ordered the Jesuits and the Indians to leave the mission, and when asked why has stated, "They must learn to submit to the will of God." When told by the Indian chief that he doesn't think the cardinal speaks for God, but instead for the Portuguese, the cardinal replies, "I do not personally speak for God, but I do speak for the Church, which is God's instrument on earth."

To claim that the church is God's instrument on earth is a sword that cuts both ways. Theologically speaking, the cardinal's claim is quite correct. The church *is* God's instrument on earth. But given the specific context, in which the church has abandoned the Guarani and has thereby allied itself with the forces of domination in order to guarantee its own power and influence elsewhere throughout the world, the cardinal's claim implies hypocrisy and exclusivity that is incompatible with the activity of God as revealed in Jesus of Nazareth. The church is indeed created by the Spirit and "called out" by Christ to be a witness, model, and agent of God's liberation and community in all the world. But the church must exercise caution that it does not set itself up as the definitive and exclusive bearer of God's activity in the world. To fail to recognize this tension is to fail to recognize that the church is called to be holy, but that we ourselves are not the source of that holiness. The holiness of the church always lies outside itself.

The Church Catholic

The word "catholic" in the Apostles' Creed does not refer specifically to the Roman Catholic Church as a Christian fellowship, but to the quality of catholicity, or universality, which is a central mark of the church. To speak of the holy church as also a catholic church is to hold that the church fails to be the church when it erects barriers to open and full participation in its life and ministry. So, also, the word *catholic*, which derives from the Greek phrase "on the whole," can mean united, undivided, or entire. To be a catholic church is to embrace our brothers and sisters in Christ throughout the world, regardless of denomination or culture—and to embrace them body and soul, that is, in their entirety.

As with holiness, so also catholicity is a gift of the Holy Spirit. Just as the story of the tower of Babel narrates the fracturing of human community through the diversity of language (Gen. 11:1–9), so Pentecost tells the story of a new creation where each person hears the gospel in his or her own language (Acts 2:6).[21] The presence of the Spirit creates the church as an inclusive and universal community, but these twin qualities of inclusiveness and universality must be held in careful tension.

On the one hand, the universality of the Spirit, expressed so well in Peter's quotation from the prophet Joel ("I will pour out my spirit on all flesh" [RSV]), is the foundation for precisely the kind of global evangelization that drives the church into the world and that stands behind the Jesuit missions in Latin America. As we have already seen with the ascension, to be faithful to Christ is to be a people who are sent on a mission. In fact, in Robert Bolt's screenplay for *The Mission*, Father Gabriel was originally to have died celebrating mass inside the mission chapel as the fiery ceilings gave way and collapsed onto the worshipers below. Father Berrigan, however, advised the filmmakers that this ending distorted the true nature of the church, and so he worked with them to refashion the final scene, keeping in mind Martin Luther King, Jr.'s, famous dictum, "The Church is the place you go from."[22] So it is that the film instead depicts Father Gabriel's death while he is leading the people of God from the church out into the world, albeit nonviolently, with only the eucharist in his hands. In a church that takes seriously its call to be catholic, all doors open outward.

At the same time, however, if the church's sense of universality becomes translated into a sense of superiority, domination, or authority, then it has misunderstood universality as vocation and task and instead turned it into an oppressive, even demonic, abstract principle. *The Mission*, for example, depicts some of the Guarani Indians as having been included in the Jesuit order. One of them has even been appointed superior of a mission. In fact, however, the Jesuits decided early in the actual history of their missions among the Guarani that "no Indian was capable of becoming a member of the Order." Insofar as the Indians were held to be "incapable of abstract thought," they were "apt only to imitate European artifacts, calligraphy, and architecture."[23] This failure of the church to wholeheartedly embrace the Guarani stands in striking contrast, of course, with the depiction of the Guarani themselves, who accept their former enemy, Rodrigo Mendoza, into the heart of their community, despite what he has done to them.

Once again, we must remember that catholicity is a creation of the Holy Spirit and can only be realized by a church that is open and loyal to the Holy Spirit. The church has traditionally had little difficulty in attempting to assert its universality, even to the point of killing, excommunicating, or libeling fellow Christians who are taken as "rivals." But how easy it is for the church to forget its inclusiveness and instead to give in to the world's standards of what is acceptable and practical. So, for example, it is said—and rightly so—that the single hour from 11:00 to 12:00 each week on Sunday morning is the most segregated hour in America. The church often justifies its segregation and fragmentation on the basis of being "realistic" and "pragmatic." Some church growth theorists have even proposed that this homogeneity is a good thing, advising churches to adopt it as a principle for mission and evangelism. This is the way the world is; "birds of a feather flock together." But perhaps we would do well to remember the final exchange between Cardinal Altamirano and Señor Hontar:

> *Hontar:* We had no alternative, your eminence. We must work in the world. The world is thus.
>
> *Altamirano:* No, Señor Hontar, thus have we made the world. Thus have I made it.

The Church Militant, the Church Triumphant

A long-standing distinction in Christian theology is that of "the church militant" and "the church triumphant." The latter refers to the saints who have already died and gone on before us, those who make up that "great cloud of witnesses" that surround us in the race we are running (Heb. 12:1). The "church militant," on the other hand, refers to the church that is still "fighting," so to speak, in the struggle to see God's will be done on earth as it in heaven. *Militant* is a rather violent term, but in the context of *The Mission*, it is not difficult to see how Gabriel and Rodrigo both represent the church militant, the church engaged in a struggle for liberation and community. Indeed, a significant segment of the church would affirm with Father Gabriel that a single act of nonviolent resistance is ultimately far more powerful a force than all the brute strength that can be summoned by the world's greatest armies.

The importance of the church triumphant for those of us who still live and work in the church militant must never be overlooked. Indeed, *The Mission* powerfully raises just this question of how the dead shall be remembered by the living. Not all Christians agree on the role of "saints" in the life of the church. Some Christians, for example, hold that Christian saints should be fondly remembered. They may even believe that qualities of their lives may be imitated or held up as examples for our own lives. Other Christians practice veneration of the saints and understand them as intercessors to God on our behalf.

Wherever we stand on our understanding of saints, however, we lose something extraordinarily important for what it means to be the church if we lose the larger sense of corporate life together that spans not only the globe but also time.[24] In our rush to be relevant and contemporary, we may from time to time fail to remember that the church is far bigger than any one local manifestation, congregation, ministry, or denomination. In our own age, the phenomenon of denominational splintering can lead one group to believe it has the corner on the market in terms of what it means to be the church. On the other hand, the phenomenon of non-denominationalism can cause a group to believe it can merely skip over two thousand years of Christian tradition in order to retrieve authentic, apostolic Christianity. Both of these responses represent a failure to judge rightly the body of Christ (1 Cor. 11:27–29) and lead to a church that is narrow-minded and divided, concerned only with its own individual needs and desires. In *The Mission*, Cardinal Altamirano had become so attentive to the wants of a powerful church in one tiny part of the globe that he failed until it was too late to consider the needs of a powerless church in another part of the globe. In his final words, however, we may nonetheless detect a message of hope and of warning—a message that calls us as the holy catholic church to remember the church triumphant:

> "So, Holiness, now your priests are dead and I am left alive. But in truth it is I who am dead, and they who live. For as always, your Holiness, the spirit of the dead will survive in the memory of the living."

QUESTIONS FOR DISCUSSION

1. What are the different "faces" of the church that you see in this film?
2. With whom do you tend to identify more closely: Father Gabriel or Rodrigo Mendoza? Why?

3. What do you think it means to be "the church"? Can you define the word *church*?

4. Are there any lessons about the nature and mission of the church that you take away from this film?

5. How does the film treat the question of salvation and conversion?

RELATED FILMS

At Play in the Fields of the Lord (1991)
Chariots of Fire (1981)
Romero (1989)
A Man for All Seasons (1966)
Mass Appeal (1984)
The Shoes of the Fisherman (1968)

NOTES

[1]John Wesley, "Of the Church," in *The Works of John Wesley*, vol. 6 (Kansas City: Beacon Hill Press), 392.

[2]Daniel Berrigan S.J., *The Mission: A Film Journal* (San Francisco: Harper and Row, 1986), 4.

[3]Ibid., 16.

[4]Ibid., 18–19.

[5]Roger Ebert describes the film as follows: "Two great colonial forces are competing for the hearts and minds of the native Indians. On the one hand, there are the imperialist plunderers, who want to establish a trade in riches and slaves. On the other hand, there are the missionaries, who want to convert the Indians to Christ." *Chicago Sun-Times*, November 14, 1986.

[6]Paulo Freire, *Pedagogy of the Oppressed* (New York: Crossroad, 1983), 151.

[7]See, for example, *At Play in the Fields of the Lord* (1991), a similarly interesting film about the lack of cultural sensitivity of a group of evangelical missionaries who are working among the Amazonian Indians.

[8]Berrigan, 11.

[9]Ibid., 11–12.

[10]Alfred Loisy, *The Gospel and the Church* (Buffalo: Prometheus, 1988), 145. Loisy most likely did not mean this as a criticism of the church, however.

[11]Jennings, *Loyalty to God*, 181.

[12]Marthaler, *The Creed*, 279.

[13]"However far we go back in the sequence of confessions of faith or creeds, we find the article on the Church linked to that on the Holy Spirit." Yves Congar, *I Believe in the Holy Spirit*, vol. 2 (New York: Seabury Press, 1983), 5.

[14]Jennings, 180.

[15]Cranfield, *The Apostles' Creed*, 60.

[16]Ephesians 5:27; 1 Peter 2:5, 9.

[17]Jennings, 187.

[18]Ibid., 186–87.

[19]Dietrich Bonhoeffer, *The Cost of Discipleship* (New York: Simon & Schuster, 1995), 44–45.

[20]Jennings, 182–83.

[21]Ibid., 185.

[22]Berrigan, 43.

[23]Ibid., 108.

[24]"Catholicity is a matter both of time and of place." Cranfield, 63.

12

"The communion of saints"

 *Babette's Feast*

There is an old parable that describes the difference between heaven and hell. The inhabitants of hell, so the story goes, are seated together around a huge pot of exquisite stew tragically separated from them by an uncrossable chasm. Each of the residents of hell is provided a spoon with a handle long enough to reach the stew, but the handle is so long and the stew so far away that it is impossible to return any of it to their mouths. This is their torment day and night—to be able to smell and even dip into the most delightful stew ever made, but without ever being able to taste it. Heaven, surprisingly enough, is said to offer precisely the same accommodations. The residents are separated from the stew by a wide chasm and are likewise provided spoons with handles long enough to reach it but too long to return any of it to their mouths. The difference, however, is that in heaven the saints are feeding each other.

As we saw in the previous chapter, authentic Christian faith, while always deeply personal, can never be entirely individualistic or private without great loss to faith itself. At the heart of Christian faith is the experience of community and fellowship—a communion with those who share the same loyalties and allegiances. The Apostles' Creed speaks of this as the "communion of saints." The phrase is not merely a different way of making the same point that we saw in the previous phrase, "holy catholic church." Something new and very important is at stake here.

The sharing of food is a fitting image for expressing this reality of Christian community and fellowship. There is something about eating a meal together that can express—and create—a sense of companionship and camaraderie. We should not be surprised to find that the central rituals of both Judaism and Christianity take place around a meal—the Jewish Passover and the Christian eucharist, or Lord's supper. In fact, it is actually quite amazing just how central the sharing of food is to the entire biblical narrative, from Genesis to Revelation. Two of Jesus' most important miracles center on food—his first miracle, in Cana, is the making of wine, and, of course, he is also recorded as having fed a group of more than five thousand people from a mere five loaves and two fishes. It is the eating habits of Jesus, in fact, that cause many of the controversies that dog him throughout his ministry. He enjoys table fellowship with sinners, tax collectors, and prostitutes and bids his disciples to do the same. He describes the kingdom of God as a great banquet in which those who are allegedly God's friends fail to show up, so the master must send out into the streets and dirt roads for the poor, the weak, and the powerless. It is they who become the esteemed dinner guests in the kingdom.

After Jesus' resurrection, two of his appearances center on food. In one, he shows up on the shores of the Sea of Galilee frying up some fish for his disciples. In another, he walks unrecognized with two of his disciples to the village of Emmaus. It is not until he breaks bread that they finally recognize who he is. The book of Acts records that one of the signal qualities of the New Testament church after Pentecost was the fact that they broke bread together from house to house, taking their meals in common. And, finally, in the book of Revelation, we find that the future of the people of God is described in terms of a wedding banquet.

The tradition of utilizing the imagery of a shared meal to communicate the mysterious experience of transformation and acceptance at the heart of the communion of saints is continued in the delightful film *Babette's Feast*. Directed by Gabriel Axel, this adaptation of the short story by Isak Dineson (*Out of Africa*) won the Academy Award for Best Foreign Film for 1987. Babette (played splendidly by Stephane Audran) is a talented French chef who flees the atrocities of the 1871 Communard uprising in her native Paris to an isolated coastal village on the Jutland coast of Denmark. Babette is taken in as a cook and housekeeper in return for lodging by two pious sisters who, along with the rest of the villagers, are unaware of her exceptional culinary skills.

The sisters, Martina (Birgitte Federspiel) and Philippa (Bodil Kjer), are the spiritual leaders of a small puritanical sect begun by their austere and deeply religious father (the sisters were even named after Martin Luther, the great Protestant reformer, and Philip Melancthon, the theologian who followed Luther). The other members of the community are likewise ascetic, strict, and exclusive. Throughout the film the photography of the windswept, Jutland coast is every bit as bleak as the lifestyle of the villagers themselves.

The two sisters have devoted their lives to continuing the work of their now deceased father, giving up careers and would-be suitors along the way. Philippa, for example, has a beautiful voice that once attracted the attention of French opera singer Achille Papin, who happened to be visiting Jutland. In a flashback scene, Papin convinces young Philippa to take music lessons from him so her voice would be better able to praise God. As he goes about the lessons, he recognizes her talent and promises her a magnificent future in the opera houses of Paris. The relationship is doomed before it really has time to commence, however, when the father overhears the two practicing a passionate love duet from Mozart's *Don Giovanni*. Even the music in the lives of this strict community avoids any association with the sensual and the worldly. Likewise, when handsome cavalry officer Löwenhielm makes advances toward young Martina, the stern father reels her back into the world-denying asceticism of the isolated community. It is not the demands of this world but of another that must retain the attention of those who are truly devoted to God.

The pastor finally dies, but Philippa and Martina remain in the house, seeing to the needs of the congregation and attempting to maintain the spiritual integrity of the community. The group meets weekly in the home of Martina and Philippa, continuing the religious traditions begun by their father and revering his memory. Over the years, however, the small community has become increasingly engulfed in bitterness, jealousy, and guilt. They hold grudges against one another and harbor resentments that just seem to fester.

For fourteen years Babette graciously serves the two sisters and their ever-diminishing community, never asking for a thing. She readily accepts the task of preparing the meals for the community's weekly services, and she continues the sisters' tradition of delivering food to the needy of the community. In keeping with the puritanical lifestyle of the community, however, Babette is allowed only to make the blandest of foods—smoked cod and a staple known as ale bread: bread soaked in beer and water and then cooked into a gruel. Babette never once begrudges the assignment or offers a complaint.

One day, Babette receives word that she has won ten thousand francs in a lottery. She decides to prepare an extravagant French meal for the entire community on the one-hundreth anniversary of the birth of Martina and Philippa's father. The sisters resist, but Babette begs them to allow her just this one privilege. Of course, many of the foods are far too exquisite—even sinful—in the eyes of the aging and sensually uptight members of the community. They fear for their own spiritual well-being. Not wishing to hurt her feelings or reject her good intentions, however, they agree to eat the meal, but determine not to allow themselves to really enjoy it. The food may pass through their lips, but their spirits will be elsewhere. Needless to say, they are all in for a grand surprise.

Babette's Feast
© Orion Pictures Corporation, Courtesy MoM/A

Babette lets out all the stops. Imported into her kitchen are all sorts of sumptuous food and exquisite drink: turtle soup, *Blenis*

Demidoff, quail stuffed with truffles, *foie gras*, *baba au rhum*, and *Veuve Clicquot*. The table is elegantly prepared, and the dinner guests are summoned to begin. By coincidence, a much older Löwenhielm, now a decorated general, has been invited along with his aunt as a dinner guest for this occasion. Having spent time in some of the fanciest restaurants in Paris, it is he who recognizes Babette's virtuoso artwork and is overflowing with praise and admiration.

Though the general is the only visitor who is able to fully taste the grace and beauty of this seven-course meal (one of the dinner guests crassly mistakes the champagne for lemonade), there is a growing awareness among all the table guests that they have been treated to something quite extraordinary. More is going on during the meal than the mere satisfaction of appetite. Those who are gathered at the dinner table begin gradually to overcome their apprehensions about the feast and to experience joy and communion as they extend acceptance to one another and begin to forgive each other for sins committed long ago. Though the film develops slowly, the beautiful scenes of walls being broken down and relationships being mended around the table are well worth the wait. As the film draws to a close, the villagers go out of the house rejoicing and join hands in a circle as they sing a hymn of praise. They nod and smile together, affirming each other and the world God has allowed them to enjoy. They have experienced spontaneous, sacrificial, and extravagant love, and they are unable to do anything but respond with joy and acceptance.

All these qualities of authentic Christian community, such as confession and forgiveness, restoration and healing, joy and celebration, give *Babette's Feast* a quality that is literally brimming with theological significance. In applying the film to a theology of Christian community, we must pay especially close attention to the roles played by Babette, the meal, and General Löwenhielm.

Babette, the Christ-Figure

It is possible to get so lost in the powerful picture of community that is depicted in the closing moments of this film that Babette, the one who makes this community possible through her gracious and sacrificial gift, is lost or forgotten. The relationship of Babette to the community gathered around the table can be viewed as an allegory of Christ's relationship to the church. The church is a community of people who joyously accept, forgive, and nurture one another, but their coming together at all is only made possible by the lavish gift of Christ.

In his outstanding book *Imaging the Divine*, Lloyd Baugh makes the case that Babette functions as a Christ-figure in the film.[1] Baugh compares the story of Christ's submission and sacrificial gift for the salvation of others with Babette's life. Babette arrives as a stranger in Jutland and, though she is a renowned chef, submits to cooking cod and ale-bread for fourteen years. She cannot speak the language and is penniless. She is a refugee, dependent wholly on the mercies of others; she is a servant who takes her meals alone in the kitchen. The feast is Babette's last hurrah, and through her total and unselfish sacrifice she paves the way for restoration and salvation to a community that is rife with bitterness and fear. Babette has so willingly emptied herself into this meal, in fact, that one could say that, like Christ's presence in the eucharist, it is Babette's own substance that is being consumed by those around the table.

Baugh sees in the contrast between the cold, theocratic leadership of the pastor-father and the warm, extravagant self-offering of Babette a symbol of the transition from the old covenant to the new—a transition from law to grace.[2] It is this broader history of salvation against which it becomes possible to see the full significance of the Christ-figure. The meal, as we shall have occasion to talk more about later, is an image of the Last Supper (not coincidentally, there are twelve in attendance). It is, indeed, an *agape* meal—a love feast and sacrament of grace. Babette has no ulterior motives. She seeks nothing for herself. She could easily have spent the entire ten thousand francs on herself. The motivation for Babette's offering is sheer excess; it is, in the fullest sense of the word, a mystery provided for the benefit of others. It is sacrificial and unnecessary. It is grace.

Throughout Christian history, theologians have attempted to describe Christ's work for the benefit of the world in various ways. Christ is a *priest* who offers the ultimate sacrifice as an atonement for sin. Christ is a *prophet* who proclaims a revolutionary message that inspires hope and turns the world upside down. Christ is a *king* who conquers the powers of evil and triumphs over death. In *Babette's*

Feast we discover the image of Christ as *artist*. Babette does not merely work over a hot stove to feed her friends because she wants to serve them and do something nice for them. Her motivation is much deeper. She is an artist. What she provides through her culinary art is a vehicle for offering her very own self to the community—for, as with all good art, the meal is quite literally an extension of Babette. Though she spends all she has on the meal, she is not depleted or impoverished. She is made rich, as is the community that benefits from her art. As Babette says, "An artist is never poor." In *Babette's Feast*, we are witnessing one of the most exquisite depictions of grace and one of the most revealing Christ-figures ever portrayed.

The Meal as Sacrament

There are two rather unfortunate trends in contemporary Christianity. They are the dual tendencies, first, to over-privatize and, second, to over-spiritualize the experience of new life in Christ. This is especially true in Western cultures, where a rank individualism both fuels and is fueled by the drive to personally acquire, consume, climb, and hoard more than the next person (which, in turn, becomes the definition of success). In a world of personal checking, personal body trainers, and personal computers, the Christian faith has become a religion of personal acceptance of Jesus Christ—the end product of something called "personal evangelism." Conversion is a private transaction between the individual and God, and the Christian journey is a solitary road down which the believer and Jesus travel hand in hand. Running parallel to this privatization is a spiritualization that shifts the believer's sights away from this world and toward another and couches faith in wholly non-materialistic terms. Christian faith no longer conflicts with materialism and consumerism, because it has become unhinged from responsibility to the world. The values of the kingdom no longer conflict with the values of the world.

What we find in *Babette's Feast*, however, is the triumph of the physical as a vehicle of the spiritual—in other words, food and drink as sacrament. William Temple, Archbishop of Canterbury, once said, "Christianity is the most materialist of all great religions."[3] He was right. The fellowship at the heart of the communion of saints is both corporate and corporeal (bodily). It is a communion that is mediated by the tangible. In authentic Christianity, all dualisms are discarded. As General Löwenhielm says of Babette, "This woman, this head chef had the ability to transform a dinner into a kind of love affair…a love affair that made no distinction between bodily appetite and spiritual appetite."

There is great irony here and, indeed, in the whole Christian notion of what it means to be a communion of saints. The small community in *Babette's Feast* promises to block all bodily sensation and enjoyment at the meal. "We shall use our tongues for prayer," says one. "It will be as if we never had the sense of taste," says another. And, as if to miss altogether the sacramental nature of Jesus' first miracle, one of the community members states, "Like the wedding at Cana, the food is of no importance." Something tragic has occurred here. The more spiritual we attempt to be, and the more we try to divorce ourselves from that which is physical, the less spiritual we actually become. In *Babette's Feast*, we discover that spirit divorced from the body yields only a pale, emaciated existence devoid of life, joy, and salvation. When Babette serves the community rich drink and succulent flesh, the spirit is provided texture, and community is now possible. So also, when we celebrate the Lord's supper today, we do more than merely "remember" what Christ has done; we actually receive Christ's presence. The Christian vision of salvation is always thoroughly communal and utterly sacramental.

General Löwenhielm: Just Who Are the Saints?

It is interesting to note the relationship between Löwenhielm and the others at the table. Though well respected, his presence at Babette's feast is scandalous because he, an outsider to the community, is the one who actually recognizes and sings the praises of the source of this beautiful meal. It is he alone who fully grasps what a wonderful meal this is. Those who ought to be in a position to recognize grace when they experience it do not!

The phrase "I believe in the communion of saints" in the creed has been subject to several primary lines of interpretation over the centuries. Some see in the phrase a declaration that we are surrounded by a great cloud of fellow Christians (Heb. 12:1) that reaches beyond the grave and includes those saints who have gone on before us, "the church triumphant" mentioned in the previous chapter. Thus, there is a cosmic communion of the faithful that transcends death and spans the entire globe. Others find in the words a reference to the holiness of Christians (since the word *saint* literally means "holy person"), either in terms of our individual moral behavior or in terms of our incorporation into Christ's body, the church, through our participation in the liturgy and sacraments. Theodore Jennings makes the case that while all these interpretations presuppose that the clause is referring to the church, originally it had a much broader reference:

> This clause of the creed is found for the first time in a commentary by Nicetas of Remesiana in the fourth century. Thus, the clause appears together with the initial interpretation of its meaning. Nicetas says that the communion of saints refers to all just persons: "From the beginning of the world patriarchs, prophets, martyrs and all other just men who have lived, are living or who will live in the time to come."[4]

If Jennings is right, this simple little phrase in the creed may well be the most controversial. It may be that we completely miss the true significance of what it means to be a communion of saints when we presume that the church is the exclusive bearer of the kingdom of God and the sole context for salvation in the world. The communion of saints transcends the artificial line between church and nonchurch, those who know and acknowledge the lordship of Jesus and those who do not. It instead points to "an intimate relation between persons whether within or without the Church, a solidarity based on their commitment to the justice of God."[5]

Think back now to General Löwenhielm's role at Babette's feast. The general is the only one at the table who does not know the source of the meal, and yet this does not preclude his ability to enjoy it, participate in it, and even receive the communal salvation extended by it. In fact, though he alone does not know the chef is Babette, it is he alone who is able to recognize in the meal its value and beauty. It is he alone who perceives the exorbitance of the grace extended to the dinner guests.

> There comes a time when your eyes are opened.
> And we come to realize that mercy is infinite.
> We need only await it with confidence and receive it in gratitude.
> Mercy imposes no conditions.
> And, lo! Everything we have chosen has been granted to us.
> And everything we rejected has also been granted.
> Yes, we even get back what we rejected.
> For mercy and truth are met together.
> And righteousness and bliss shall kiss one another.

How is it that this outsider is able to recognize and experience the very mercy and gratitude about which the small community of faith seems only able to sing? We are reminded once again of Jesus' judgment parable mentioned in chapter 9, where the sheep were distinguished from the goats by a startling set of criteria that placed the focus on one's life-activity, commitments, and allegiances rather than on more customary religious criteria. Both the sheep and the goats were surprised to discover their true identity. Neither realized what their life-activity had counted for or how it had either suc ceeded or failed in knowing God. So also, for Jesus, it is the ones who do God's will who belong to the communion of saints, and the ones who do not do God's will are excluded from that fellowship, even while the Lord's name is on their very lips (Mt. 7:21). This means that "true religion is not only found in the Church, but also before and outside the Church, indeed wherever we find a commitment to the will of God and a life of truth and love."[6] Archbishop Oscar Romero stated it this way: "Everyone who struggles for justice, everyone who makes just claims in unjust surroundings, is working for God's reign, even though not a Christian. The Church does not comprise all of God's reign; God's reign goes beyond the Church's boundaries."[7] The communion of saints extends to all those who will participate in Christ's banquet of "kin"-dom, sharing, joy, and acceptance. Hallelujah!

Questions for Discussion

1. What does this film communicate to you about the nature of true community and fellowship?
2. What is the role of Babette in the film? How do you see her in relationship to the other central characters?
3. Why is it that the meal had such powerful transforming effects on the community that was gathered together to eat it?
4. Does the character of General Löwenhielm, especially his presence at the dinner table, have any special significance in the film that you can see?
5. The Apostles' Creed follows up the phrase "I believe in the holy catholic church" with the phrase, "I believe in the communion of saints." Is this just a redundancy or is there something else being communicated here?

Related Films

Big Night (1996)
The Dream Team (1989)
Grand Canyon (1991)
Marvin's Room (1996)
The Mission (1986)

Notes

[1]Baugh, *Imaging the Divine*, 137–45.
[2]Ibid., 138–39.
[3]William Temple, *Readings in St. John's Gospel*, vol. 1 (London: MacMillan, 1939).
[4]Jennings, *Loyalty to God*, 194.
[5]Ibid., 195.
[6]Ibid.
[7]Quoted in The Church is All of You: Thoughts of Archbishop Oscar Romero, compiled and translated by James R. Brockman (Minneapolis: Winston Press, 1984), 38.

13

"The forgiveness of sins"

 *Dead Man Walking*

Go to any prison and ask the inhabitants, who have written shameful lines across the pages of their lives. From behind the bars they will tell you that society is slow to forgive. Make your way to death row and speak with the tragic victims of criminality. As they prepare to make their pathetic walk to the electric chair, their hopeless cry is that society will not forgive. Capital punishment is society's final assertion that it will not forgive.[1]

With these words, Martin Luther King, Jr., contrasts Jesus' prayer from the cross ("Father, forgive them; for they do not know what they are doing") with our human tendency to be slow to forgive and quick to seek revenge. As much as any Christian in recent time, King both understood and practiced the centrality of forgiveness in the Christian life, especially the forgiveness of enemies. It is precisely this capacity for forgiving others, along with the experience of being forgiven, that is at the center of what it means to be the communion of saints who live in the domain of the Holy Spirit. And yet nowhere is the ability to forgive and to receive forgiveness tested as radically as in the case of the one who sits on death row, the one who is considered "unforgivable."

On the face of it, Tim Robbins' *Dead Man Walking* (1995) may appear to be a story that asks primarily about the morality of the death penalty. It is difficult to watch the film without being transported into that complicated debate. Ultimately, however, the film is about much more than this. It is about redemption and unconditional love. It is a story about forgiveness and how ordinary human beings can both experience forgiveness and be the agents of forgiveness.

Dead Man Walking is based on a book of the same name written by Sister Helen Prejean, who recounts her experiences with death row inmates in Louisiana's Angola State Prison. Sister Helen, who comes from a comfortable, middle-class background, lives in a poor, inner-city neighborhood in New Orleans where she teaches adult literacy. Through a course of events she could not have predicted, she ends up corresponding with a death row inmate and eventually serves as his spiritual advisor in the days leading up to his execution. As Prejean says in the introduction to her book,

> I've heard that there are two situations that make interesting stories: when an extraordinary person is plunged into the commonplace and when an ordinary person gets involved in extraordinary events. I'm definitely an example of the latter.[2]

This hesitancy and lack of pretension on Sister Helen's part is caught beautifully on screen by Susan Sarandon, who received an Academy Award for her understated and credible portrayal of Sister Helen.[3] Through Sarandon's performance, we see Sister Helen transformed into a woman who learns about her own faith and courage as she not only provides friendship and comfort to a brutal rapist and murderer, but ultimately gets him to acknowledge his own responsibility and need for forgiveness.

Sister Helen's visit to Angola is her first time in a prison, and it is clear she is in foreign territory. The prison chaplain is a priest who has become hardened over the years and sees himself as the "experienced hand," in contrast to which he sees Sister Helen as a naïve bleeding heart who can easily be manipulated by the convicts and who is clearly out of her depth. The chaplain warns her, "There is no romance here, Sister…they are all con men and they will take advantage of you every way they can." Throughout the film, the chaplain (who is also a real-life character from Sister Helen's experience) comes off as cynical and inauthentic, as one who is more concerned with the fact that Sister Helen is not properly dressed as a nun than with genuine concern for the inmates.

Sean Penn provides an equally powerful performance, maybe his best ever, as Matthew Poncelet, a white, racist inmate in his sixth month on death row, convicted for the murder of a teenage boy and the brutal rape and murder of his girlfriend. Poncelet, who comes from a very poor family ("There's no one with money on death row," he accurately states), is actually a composite of two killers for whom Sister Helen served as spiritual advisor. Poncelet's wariness and foul-

Dead Man Walking: © Gramercy Pictures, Courtesy MoMA

mouthed, insulting behavior in the beginning of the film eventually give way to respect and contrition as his relationship with Sister Helen develops in the days leading up to his execution. Penn makes the transformation believable, accomplishing the amazing task of causing viewers both to despise him at some points and feel sympathy for him at others.

With Sister Helen's help, Poncelet manages to engage an able lawyer to represent him at his clemency hearing and in front of the governor, though both to no avail. At the hearing, Sister Helen meets the victims' parents, Earl Delacroix and Clyde and Mary Beth Percy. Robbins allows the full expression of their pain mingled with anger to be vented on screen, especially toward Sister Helen. In this way, the viewer is never left to consider the death penalty in the abstract, apart from the real-life consequences that such a horrible crime leaves in its wake. They criticize Sister Helen for not having visited them and for instead coming to Poncelet's defense. Delacroix, who is Roman Catholic, especially takes offense at what he perceives to be Sister Helen's preferential option for victimizers rather than the victims.

Poncelet's lawyer attempts to portray him before the hearing board as a human being rather than a monster. "It's easy to kill a monster; it's hard to kill a human being." This theme recurs throughout the movie. On the one hand, the Percys refer to Poncelet as "a monster," "scum," "God's mistake," "the enemy," and "an animal." Sister Helen, on the other hand, is intent on finding the humanity in Matthew Poncelet, however distorted and hidden that might be. As she says to the Percys, "I'm just trying to follow the example of Jesus who said that every person is worth more than their worst act."[4]

That humanity is often difficult to locate, however. Poncelet has become adept at lying, shifting blame, and playing the role of the "tough guy." At one point he even makes advances toward Sister Helen, though she quickly sets him straight. The film enhances the unfolding of their relationship and the transformation of Poncelet by skillful camera work with the grilles, bars, and Plexiglas screens used in an actual prison setting. In some scenes, we actually see both of their faces at the same time as one face is looking through the clear screen and the other's reflection appears next to it. Also, initially, a thick mesh grille separates the two, but as the film progresses, the barriers become increasingly transparent until finally, in the walk to Poncelet's execution, they disappear altogether, and Sister Helen is actually able to make physical contact by placing her hand on his shoulder.

In the execution scene, Poncelet is strapped upright to the table where the lethal injection will be administered, his arms outstretched. He is then exposed in cruciform position to the witnesses and family members in the observation room. Robbins has been criticized for using the overt crucifixion imagery at this point and of attempting to inappropriately portray Poncelet as a "Christ-figure."[5] In an interview, however, Robbins explains that he is only being true to the actual arrangements.

"I knew that people would look at the execution scene— the way in which Poncelet gets strapped to the table, with his arms spread out like Jesus on the cross—and think I was trying to make some kind of parallel, which I'm not doing at all. This is really the way the table is made. At first, it is in an upright position…It's much easier to walk him in, to strap him in while he stands, to take his handcuffs off and only then to bring him back into the horizontal position. We made none of that stuff up; it's all meticulously researched."[6]

In order also to prevent us from making the inference that Poncelet is a Christ-figure, Robbins includes a scene where Poncelet actually compares his own execution to that of Jesus. Sister Helen quickly prevents him from moving down that path, however. Jesus "changed the world with love," she says, while "you watched those two young people be murdered."

Few scenes in cinematic history are as powerful as the final scenes in Poncelet's life, including not only his confession and finding forgiveness, but the walk from his cell to the execution room and the intercut scenes of the murders with Poncelet's execution. At one point, Poncelet can barely stand up on his way to the execution room. Sister Helen kneels next to him, telling him to look into her face as "they do this thing," so that the last face he sees is "a face of love." Sister Helen is for him the incarnation of strength, compassion, hope, and love. "Christ is here," she says. Sister Helen is right.

Embodying Forgiveness[7]

One of the most profound links between the New Testament and *Dead Man Walking* is their portrayals of the intricate relationship between the act of forgiving and the act of receiving forgiveness. *Dead Man Walking* is the story of two struggles: the struggle of Matthew Poncelet to find forgiveness and the struggle of others (including society itself) over whether and how to offer forgiveness. Likewise, throughout the New Testament the command to forgive others is almost always tied directly to our own experience of being forgiven. Jesus, in what is often called "the Lord's Prayer," bids us to pray as follows: "forgive us our debts as we also have forgiven our debtors" (Mt. 6:12). Although many Christians know this entire prayer by heart, Jesus' statement that immediately follows this prayer is not as well known, "For if you forgive [people] for their transgressions, your heavenly Father will also forgive you. But if you do not forgive [people], then your Father will not forgive your transgressions" (6:14, 15). This is strong language,[8] but there is no way of getting around it. Our experience of forgiveness is intimately related to and dependent on our practice of forgiving others. The two rise and fall together.

This core Christian belief in the two-way relationship between offering forgiveness and experiencing forgiveness is not always factored into the discussion on capital punishment by Christians who engage in that debate. Often the discussion turns on what the perpetrator of the crime deserves or what is best for society. Christians must certainly engage in such debates, but the starting point for the Christian response is always a forgiveness that springs from nothing less than the mere fact that we ourselves have been forgiven. Neither can the repentance of the offender be somehow required as the trigger that causes us now to forgive where once we would not. As Christians, we forgive merely because we have been forgiven. One may certainly ask what it means practically to "embody" the forgiveness of someone like a murderer or rapist; certainly the concrete form in which such forgiveness is expressed will require creativity, courage, and careful reflection. But the fact that we begin with a persistent[9] forgiveness and the fact that our practice of forgiveness is intimately related to our own experience of forgiveness is, in the New Testament, beyond dispute.

Clearly the cost of embodying such forgiveness is extraordinarily high, as we can see in the experience of Sister Helen. It may mean being ostracized by a world (and by fellow Christians!) for whom the practice of forgiveness is perceived as irrational or a failure of nerve, a weakness rather than strength. Because the cost is so high, some Christians, as Gregory Jones notes, may "invent and turn to cheaper versions of forgiveness, ones that will enable them to 'feel' or 'think' better about themselves—or simply to 'cope' with their situation—without having to engage in struggles to change or transform the patterns of their relationships."[10]

We find this sort of "cheapening" of forgiveness in the case of the prison chaplain in *Dead Man Walking*. As he says to Sister Helen, "This boy is to be executed in six days, and is in dire need of redemption…You can save this boy by getting him to receive the sacraments of the Church before he dies. This is your job. Nothing more. Nothing less." The chaplain has reduced forgiveness to a mechanical transaction that takes place outside both the giver and receiver of forgiveness. Nothing in the chaplain's relationship to Poncelet is required to change or be affected by the extending of this forgiveness, and he seems not to care whether anything really happens within Poncelet's own mind, body, and spirit. In other words, there is no "embodying" of forgiveness.[11] In fact, the chaplain makes it very clear that he has given up on Poncelet and, for that matter, on all the convicts in Angola. In a sense, his attitude is not unlike the poster that, according to Sister Helen, was kept on display in the home of one of the victims' families: "Tell them about Jesus, then put them in the electric chair!"[12] Lest this criticism of the chaplain be perceived as little more than a Protestant criticism of the Roman Catholic emphasis on the sacrament as a cheapening of forgiveness, it is worth noting that Protestants have been equally guilty of reducing forgiveness to an un-"embodied" mental transaction under the guise of "faith." As was noted in chapter 6, it is relatively easy to ask someone "to accept Jesus as your personal savior" with no apparent context or spelling out of what that might mean in terms of loyalties and values. To the extent that "getting saved" or "being born again" is a simple transaction that takes place in a matter of seconds and requires nothing more than a quick trip to the altar or the flipping of a mental switch, we find a *cheapening* of forgiveness that may eventually result in an *eclipse* of forgiveness.

Sister Helen, in contrast to both of these distortions, is not only intent on embodying forgiveness, she is intent on seeing that Poncelet comes to an embodied experience of forgiveness himself. In other words, Sister Helen is concerned to see Poncelet come to a genuine faith that involves him at the core of his being, however much work and pain that might demand. Experiencing forgiveness will include the truth, Poncelet's owning up to his sin, and a changed response toward those he has offended—not an angry lashing out at them, but final words asking for forgiveness and a wish for their peace. The path to the "truth" that "shall set you free" is costly for Poncelet, because it is genuine. In one particular scene, Poncelet parrots the standard Christian lines he has probably heard a number of times before:"Me and God. We got everything squared away. I know Jesus died on the cross for me and I know he's going to be there to take care of me when I appear before God on the judgment day." Sister Helen responds, "Matt, redemption isn't some kind of free admission ticket that you get because Jesus paid the price. You've got to participate in your own redemption. You've got some work to do."

What Sister Helen is pointing to here is the reality that forgiveness is more than just a legal transaction between the human being and God. It is an experience that involves us at the deepest level of our being. To speak with the Apostles' Creed of believing in the forgiveness of sins, then, is to affirm not merely the absolution of individual transgressions, but the fundamental acceptance by God of who we are as persons.[13] When that happens, Sister Helen can refer to Matthew Poncelet, a rapist and a murderer, as more than just forgiven, but as "a son of God."

Forgiveness and the Church

It is no accident that the creed's statement on the forgiveness of sins appears on the heels of its affirmation of the holy catholic church and the communion of saints. In the New Testament, the forgiveness of sins is clearly located as a fundamental responsibility of the entire community of faith:

> Truly I say to you, whatever you shall bind on earth shall be bound in heaven; and whatever you loose on earth shall be loosed in heaven. Again I say to you, that if two of you agree on earth about anything that they may ask, it shall be done for them by my Father who is in heaven. For where two or three have gathered together in my name, there I am in their midst. (Mt. 18:18–20)[14]

In John 20:23, Jesus makes a similar statement, connecting forgiveness to the presence of the Holy Spirit: "Receive the Holy Spirit. If you forgive the sins of any, their sins have been forgiven them; if you retain the sins of any, they have been retained." These are amazingly bold statements about the responsibility of the church in forgiveness. As Theodore Jennings says,

> Now there is simply no way around the breathtaking audacity of this authorization. It says simply that God has

determined to be bound by the decision of the followers of Jesus. What they bind will be bound by God, what they release will be released by God. God agrees to be represented by them so that what they say and do will be true of God's word and deed.[15]

As we have already seen in the case of *Jesus of Montreal*, *The Mission*, and *Babette's Feast*, there is always the danger of idolatry here: that on the basis of this responsibility the church will elevate itself and assume a privileged, authoritarian attitude toward the world. The New Testament makes clear, however, that the one who does not forgive is not forgiven, so the church is never really in a position to withhold forgiveness or to claim that the forgiveness it offers is its own.[16]

That *Dead Man Walking* does not end with Poncelet's execution is another sign that the film is not finally about capital punishment.[17] Instead the closing shot is of Sister Helen and Earl Delacroix praying together in a church, together seeking a way not only to be better recipients of God's forgiveness, but better agents. Jesus, in his time, was often accused of exercising what was thought to be the prerogative of God only—namely, the forgiveness of sins.[18] Not only did Jesus openly acknowledge that God had given him this capacity, he also passes it along to those of us who live in loyalty to his way and in openness to his Spirit. As Sister Helen Prejean writes, "Before, I had asked God to right the wrongs and comfort the suffering. Now I know—really know—that God entrusts those tasks to us."[19]

QUESTIONS FOR DISCUSSION

1. Reflect on the character of Sister Helen Prejean in this film. Are there characteristics about her life and ministry that you believe are central to what it means to be a Christian?
2. What are your thoughts on the death penalty after watching this film? Were you changed at all? Do you think the film dealt with the issue in an evenhanded way?
3. What is the meaning of "forgiveness of sins"? Is it really possible, especially for victims and families of victims, to forgive someone like Matthew Poncelet?

RELATED FILMS

Amadeus (1984)
The Mission (1986)
Schindler's List (1993)
Spitfire Grill (1996)
Unforgiven (1992)

NOTES

[1]Martin Luther King, Jr., "Love in Action," in *Strength to Love* (Philadelphia: Fortress Press, 1963), 39.

[2]Helen Prejean, *Dead Man Walking: An Eyewitness Account of the Death Penalty in the United States* (New York: Random House, 1993), xiii.

[3]According to Roger Ebert, "Sister Helen, as played here…is one of the few truly spiritual characters I have seen in the movies. Movies about 'religion' are often only that—movies about secular organizations that deal in spirituality. It is so rare to find a movie character who truly does try to live according to the teachings of Jesus (or anyone else for that matter) that it's a little disorienting." *Chicago Sun-Times*, January 12, 1996.

[4]Though Jesus is never actually recorded as having said this, such a statement may indeed capture Jesus' teachings on sin and forgiveness, albeit in words other than his.

[5]Christy Rodgers, "Dead Man Walking," *Cineaste* 22, no. 2 (1996): 43.

[6]Roy Grundmann and Cynthia Lucia, "Between Ethics and Politics: An Interview with Tim Robbins," *Cineaste* 22, no. 2 (1996): 7.

[7]I am here indebted to the suggestive title and fine analysis of forgiveness by L. Gregory Jones in *Embodying Forgiveness: A Theological Analysis* (Grand Rapids, Mich.: Eerdmans, 1995).

[8]Repeated in Mark 11:25–26 and in the parable of the unforgiving slave in Matthew 18:21–35.

[9]"Then Peter came and said to Him, 'Lord, how often shall my brother sin against me and I forgive him? Up to seven times?' Jesus said to him, 'I do not say to you, up to seven times, but up to seventy times seven'" (Mt. 18:21).

[10]Jones, 6.

[11]As the real-life Sister Helen says of the priest, "His trust is in the ritual that it will do its work…For him, the personal, human interaction of trust and love is not part of the sacrament." Prejean, 81.

[12]Ibid., 227.

[13]According to Paul Tillich, "In relation to God, it is not the particular sin as such that is forgiven but the act of separation from God and the resistance to reunion with him. It is sin which is forgiven in the forgiving of a particular sin. The symbol of forgiveness of sins has proved dangerous because it has concentrated the mind on particular sins and their moral quality rather than on the estrangement from God and its religious quality." *Systematic Theology*, vol. 3 (Chicago: University of Chicago Press, 1963), 225.

[14]The words "binding" and "loosing" are clearly speaking of forgiveness in this context where Jesus has just dealt with what we should do if someone has sinned against us in verses 15–17. A context of forgiveness is also established by the verses immediately following this passage (vv. 21–35) where Peter asks Jesus how often we should forgive, and Jesus responds with the parable of the unforgiving slave.

[15]Jennings, *Loyalty to God*, 203.

[16]"There is never any positive command to bind. But the command to forgive is insistently underscored in the most impressive ways. Thus we do not consider two equal possibilities, but only one possibility and its 'shadow.'" Ibid., 205.

[17]Cf. Roy Anker, "Dead Man Singing," *Books & Culture* (May/June 1996): 12.

[18]Matthew 9:1–8; Mark 2:7–12; Luke 5:21–26.

[19]Prejean, 11.

14

"The resurrection of the body and the life everlasting"

 *The Shawshank Redemption*

> *"Hope is a good thing, maybe the best of things,*
> *and no good thing ever dies."*
> —Andy Dufresne

With our final two phrases in the Apostles' Creed—"the resurrection of the body" and "the life everlasting"—it appears we may have made a turn toward the future, and that we are now concerned with events that Christians believe will unfold "someday." While this is undoubtedly true, no words in the creed have more centrality for our present trust and contemporary loyalties and allegiances than these seemingly futuristic ones. That is because these two phrases attempt to describe the Christian's "hope." And hope, however forward-looking it might be, is something we live out of in the present.[1] Authentic Christian hope utterly transforms the present and gives us meaning and the strength to make a difference here and now. It is not a distraction or a narcotic; neither is it an escapist avoidance mechanism. Hope is not a way "out of" the world; it is the Christian way "into" the world.

The theme of "hope" is likewise at the center of Frank Darabont's film *The Shawshank Redemption* (1994). Adapted from a Stephen King short story, the film was only a marginal success in its initial release. The popularity of the film has steadily increased since then, however. It was the top video rental of 1995[2] and in 1999 was surprisingly rated as "the greatest movie ever made" by tens of thousands of Internet users who registered their impressions at the Internet Movie Database (IMdB), a "ground zero" for film information on the Internet. According to *The Wall Street Journal*, "That a film which had only a so-so run at the box office could find redemption in the afterlife is vivid proof of a populist revolution shaking the movie industry."[3]

The film features Tim Robbins as Andy Dufresne, a young banker who in 1947 is convicted of murdering his wife and her lover and then given two life sentences in the maximum-security Shawshank State Prison. Andy maintains that he is innocent (as do all the Shawshank inmates), and at first he does not fit in very well to

The Shawshank Redemption: © Castle Rock Entertainment, Courtesy MoMA

prison life. Andy is tough, but for the first few years he is repeatedly beaten and raped. Early on, however, Andy becomes friends with Ellis "Red" Redding (Morgan Freeman), a resourceful inmate who is able to "get things" from the outside. Red, who has already been in Shawshank for twenty years prior to Andy's arrival, narrates the film, confiding that he didn't think much of Andy the first time he looked at him: "Looked like a stiff breeze would blow him over."

At Shawshank, the violence from fellow inmates is matched only by the brutality of the prison guards and the corruption of the religious but hypocritical warden. The warden welcomes the new prisoners by giving them each a Bible and informing them, "I believe in two things: discipline and the Bible. Here you'll receive both. Put your trust in the Lord. Your ass belongs to me. Welcome to Shawshank." Over time, Red manages to get for Andy three items he requests: a six-inch rock hammer, some rocks, and a large poster of Rita Hayworth (the poster transitions to Marilyn Monroe and then to Raquel Welch over the years). Andy's hobby is carving chess pieces out of rock to pass the time. When Red first orders the rock hammer he suspects Andy may intend to use it to try to escape from Shawshank, but when he actually sees the tiny hammer he remembers thinking, "It would take a man about 600 years to tunnel under the walls with one of these."

Adept at bookkeeping, Andy eventually makes his way into the good graces of the guards by doing their taxes and providing financial advice. When the warden begins selling prison labor to the outside world, Andy keeps the books, hiding the kickbacks and laundering the money. The beatings and abuse stop. From the very beginning, Andy conveys a unique resilience of spirit and an infectious sense of hope. As Red describes him, "He had a quiet way about him. A walk and talk that just wasn't normal around here. He strolled...like a man in a park without a care or a worry in the world. Like he had on an invisible coat that would shield him from this place." When one of the new inmates breaks down sobbing on the first night and is savagely beaten to death by one of the guards, Andy asks about the man the next day and wonders whether anyone knew the man's name. The other inmates look at Andy with surprise. They see the dead man as just another number, little more than an object about which to make a bet regarding who would break down crying their first night in prison. They have adapted by caving in to their dehumanizing environment. From the outset there is something different about Andy.

Throughout his stay at Shawshank, Andy relentlessly pursues the building of a library and adult education center in the prison. After six years of pursuing funds from the state, persistently writing one letter each week, Andy finally receives some books and a small grant. In celebration, with no one around, he enters the warden's office, locks the doors behind him, and begins to play an aria from *The Marriage of Figaro* over the loudspeaker system. As Mozart soars throughout the prison yard, the inmates stop what they are doing, clearly caught off balance and moved by the music. As Red put it, "It was like some beautiful bird flapped into our drab little cage and made all those walls dissolve away. And for the briefest of moments every last man at Shawshank felt free."

The turning point in the film comes nineteen years into Andy's sentence when a new young inmate shows up with clues that prove Andy's innocence. When Andy asks the warden for help in clearing his name, the warden refuses and instead gives Andy two months in "the hole" (a small, dark chamber in solitary confinement) while silencing the new inmate by having him shot. When Andy reemerges, he appears despondent, and it seems as if his hope has finally died. He confesses to Red that he was not the husband he should have been and takes the blame for driving his wife into the arms of another man. He shares his dream of living in Mexico, fixing up a boat, and living a simple life. "Don't think about Mexico," Red warns, "because it's down there and you're in here."

Andy gives Red instructions, should he ever get out, to find a box under a black rock in a remote field near Buxton, Maine. There Red will find "something" Andy wants him to have. All this kind of talk worries Red about Andy's state of mind. It sounds like a parting conversation. When it is discovered that Andy has borrowed a length of rope from one of the inmates, and when he fails to appear the next morning for roll call, the inmates suspect the worst—until, that is, Andy is found missing. As Red concludes, "Some birds aren't meant to be caged. Their feathers are just too bright."

Resurrection of the Body

What is the source of the "reserve" power that keeps Andy going, that gives him the strength and determination to retain his humanity while those around him are losing theirs? After he receives two weeks in "the hole" for playing music over the loudspeaker, the inmates question Andy on how he survived the experience. He replies that he had Mozart to keep him company. According to Andy, we all need music so we don't forget that "there are places in the world that aren't made out of stone. That there's something inside that they can't get to. That they can't touch. That's yours." When asked to explain what he is talking about, Andy answers with one word, "hope." Red and the others who are serving life sentences, however, have learned to live without hope. As Red tells Andy, "Hope is a dangerous thing. Hope can drive a man insane. It's got no use on the inside. You'd better get used to that idea."

Commenting on this film in his recent book, *Saint Paul Returns to the Movies*, Robert Jewett reminds us that Red's outlook is strikingly similar to the view commonly held in the Greco-Roman world into which Christianity was born: "Hope was viewed in that culture as a weakling's resort, a refusal to face the difficult fate that life inevitably imposes."[4] In such a climate, characterized by despair and weighed down by the heavy sense that our lives are predetermined, perhaps even written in the stars, there was, however, an alternate source of hope—largely influenced by ancient Greek philosophy. This hope was the release through death of one's "immortal soul."

Greek thought assumed a fundamental dualism between the material world and the spiritual world, with the former being an essentially inferior and imperfect shadow of the latter. It is the spiritual world that is ultimately real, unchanging, and perfect while the earth and all that is physical or material is relatively worthless. The human person is a miniature, or microcosm, of this duality. According to Greek philosophers like Socrates and Plato, each human is endowed with an immortal soul that is imprisoned within our inferior, corrupt bodies. Our only hope for salvation, therefore, is a hope for release, or "escape" from this earthly prison. Socrates, for example, "readily and cheerfully"[5] drinks the poisonous hemlock after being condemned to death, for death brings salvation in the form of escape. He even spends his last hours conversing with his disciples about the immortality of the soul: "You are burying my body only."[6]

In the Hebrew understanding of creation, such a dualism was as impossible as the notion of salvation and hope that arose out of it. On the contrary, as we saw in chapter 3, the physical world and the human body are creations of God and essentially good. Indeed, if we can use the word *soul* at all in the Hebrew view, it must be understood as the divine breath (see chapter 10) that animates the body and is blown into us by our Creator, thereby making us living beings (Gen. 2:7). For the Hebrew, however, it would be impossible (or at best an abstraction) to talk about the soul apart from the body, just as it would be to talk about a body without a soul. Such is the wholistic view of the human person that Christianity inherited from its Jewish roots.

In contrast to the Greek view, there is, for the Hebrew, nothing about us that is essentially immortal. When we die our entire self dies: body, mind, soul, spirit, emotions, and breath. In no sense does anything about us somehow "escape" death. For that reason, death can never be viewed as salvation, nor can the Hebrew and Christian hope be properly expressed in terms of the "immortality of the soul." What is hoped for instead is the "resurrection of the body." Immortality, as the apostle Paul states, is something we mortals "put on" or are "clothed with" in the resurrection (1 Cor. 15:52–55). It is not something that characterizes us prior to that. The difference between these two worldviews has enormous consequences. While Greek thought looks on death as a friend and liberator, for the Hebrew, death is an enemy. Even though the Christian believes that death is a defeated enemy thanks to God's resurrection of Jesus, death is nonetheless real. In marked contrast to Socrates, Jesus does not look forward to death, but agonizes all night long in the garden of Gethsemane, sweating drops of blood and praying, "My Father, if it is possible, let this cup pass from me" (Mt. 26:39). Likewise, Jesus did not "swoon" on the cross. He really did die, just as we will. That, however, is why resurrection is so important. Without resurrection, we have no future.

Clearly, the Hebrew view of creation and the value it placed on the body stand in stark contrast to the Greek view so prevalent at the birth of Christianity. To the Greek mind, why the body would be of such importance and why one would hope for its resurrection was difficult to understand. Unfortunately, much of contemporary Christian thought has absorbed a dualism similar to that of the Greeks. Listen closely, for example, at a Christian funeral and consider whether the pastor tends to interpret hope more in terms of immortality of the soul or resurrection of the body. This distortion, however trivial it might seem at a funeral, can have significant consequences for how we approach ministry. Both the doctrine of creation at the front end of our theology and the doctrine of the resurrection of the body at the back end of our theology provide critically important "bookends" for our affirmation of human beings as whole persons. Christian ministry is aimed at recovering that wholeness and is directed toward all human needs, whether of the body, the mind, the spirit, or the emotions. To affirm God as the One who both creates and resurrects bodies is to reject a dualism whereby the church cares only for souls and leaves the body and mind to the care of the state or to other secular institutions.

Given this contrast between Greek and Judeo-Christian worldviews, it is clear that there are some serious problems with using *The Shawshank Redemption* as a parable for understanding Christian hope. As we have seen, the analogy of life as a prison and redemption as an escape from prison is fundamentally inadequate to the Christian vision of hope. Fortunately, *The Shawshank Redemption* is a bit more complicated than this. In the character of Andy Dufresne, we never see a preoccupation with digging tunnels or "getting out" as with so many other prison escape films.[7] Not only are his escape efforts kept a secret from us for the sake of the plot's surprise ending, they do not distract him from the here and now of prison life. If Andy were really living out of an escapist hope, he would hardly be interested in improving the conditions of prison life around him, such as building the library or working to help other inmates pass their high school equivalency exams. Andy may have been hoping, planning, and working for a way out all along, but he lives his life in the present in a way that finds hope in humanizing those around him who have become dehumanized. Andy's hope runs deeper than a mere hope for his own personal escape.

This does not change the fact, however, that the analogy of life as a prison and redemption as an escape from prison remain inadequate for our understanding of Christian hope. And yet Andy Dufresne at least proves to us that a future-oriented hope does not have to distract us from the present and can even energize our work in improving conditions here and now. Too often, as Christians, we are so preoccupied with otherworldly or next-worldly matters that the affairs of this world recede into a distant background. Evangelism then becomes a frenzied effort of filling lifeboats and getting people ready for heaven. But if Christian hope is finally escapist, then Jesus' prayer for God's kingdom to come "on earth as it is in heaven" is a mistake, and all efforts to transform society into something more closely resembling God's *shalom* are little more than the rearrangement of deck chairs on the Titanic.

For this reason, the tiny rock hammer that Andy keeps hidden within his Bible (in the pages that begin with the book of *Exodus*, by no coincidence) is one of the most compelling metaphors for hope in all of contemporary cinema.[8] Andy himself interprets it this way when he leaves the Bible in the warden's safe with an inscription that reads, "Dear Warden, you were right; salvation lies within." For Andy Dufresne, hope lies both in the fight and in the prize, both in the struggle and in the outcome, both in the present and in the future.

The Life Everlasting

If we ask about the meaning of the word *redemption* in the title *The Shawshank Redemption*, a number of possibilities present themselves. One definition of redemption is freedom from harm or captivity, so that escape from prison could be considered "redemption." More often, however, redemption means "to buy back" or "to re-purchase," so that we often find a "redemption value" printed on bottles or aluminum cans. It is in this sense that Christian salvation is spoken of in terms of "redemption," and we say that Christ has "redeemed us" (re-purchased us). Paul even speaks of resurrection as "the redemption of our bodies" (Rom. 8:23).

Naturally, there are several different ways of interpreting redemption in *The Shawshank Redemption*. In one sense, Andy has experienced redemption himself by escaping *from* Shawshank. But perhaps it is just as appropriate to say that Andy has brought redemption *to* Shawshank. It is possible, after all, to see Andy as a Christ-figure in *The Shawshank Redemption*. Innocent and meek as a lamb, he arrives in a drab and vicious world where, though clearly out of place, he assumes a life in solidarity with the other inmates. He suffers at the hands of his fellow inmates and "the powers that be." Having been crucified by the warden, he escapes by lowering himself down through the prison walls and out through the sewerage pipes (a "descent into hell"). And as Andy triumphs in the pouring rain while gazing heavenward with arms outstretched, we hear Red's amazed declaration, "Andy crawled through five hundred yards of shit and came out at the other end as fresh and clean as a newborn baby."[9] As with *Cool Hand Luke* (1967), a prison movie in which Paul Newman plays a Christ-figure, Andy's spirit of hope and passion for freedom become an inspiration for others and his life a legend that is told and retold by the inmates who are left behind. When Red is finally released, he goes to meet Andy in Mexico on a beach near the edge of the vast, blue Pacific Ocean. Andy is there to greet him.

The ocean is a wonderful metaphor for "life everlasting"—vast, unfathomable, unknowable, seemingly without end. Its warmth and beauty stand in striking contrast to the dinginess and gray of Shawshank. As Andy says, "The ocean has no memory." It is a place where both he and Red can go to leave behind the regrets and guilt of their former lives ("I am the one who wipes out your transgressions for my own sake; and I will not remember your sin," [Isa. 43:25]).

The word *redemption* is also a useful metaphor for understanding the creed's reference to "life everlasting" as a Christian symbol for hope. On the one hand, "everlasting life" is the redemption of *time* (thus the word *everlasting*), and, on the other hand, everlasting life is the redemption of *life* itself.

1. Eternal life as a "redemption of time." According to film critic Roger Ebert, "*The Shawshank Redemption* is a movie about time, patience, and loyalty."[10] Ebert is right; indeed, the entire film attempts to convey the slow, almost oppressive march of time within a prison life sentence and the "spirit-crushing boredom"[11] that accompanies it. But the film also contrasts Andy with the other prisoners precisely in how they relate to and make use of this time. Where hope has been vanquished, time within prison life is oppressive and enslaving. Red describes the first day he entered Shawshank. "Your old life is blown away in the blink of an eye," he says. "Nothing left but all the time in the world to think about it." Prison life consists of "routine and more routine."

Brooks Hatlen, the elderly prison librarian played flawlessly by James Whitmore, is a good example of the numbing effects of time without hope. Having spent fifty years behind bars, he is finally granted parole. By this time, Brooks does not want to leave prison and even fights violently to stay. Time has worked against him. As Red says, "These walls are funny. First you hate 'em. Then you get used to 'em. Enough time passes, you get so you depend on 'em." When Brooks is finally released he cannot enjoy his freedom. Without hope, Brooks eventually takes his own life.

For Andy, however, hope "redeems" time. Andy persists in mailing letters each week to the prison board requesting funds for the library, and he does this for six solid years. Of course, the most dramatic illustration of hope's redemption of time is Andy's nineteen-year-long scraping and digging through the cell block walls with his tiny rock hammer. What we see in the person of Andy Dufresne is the possibility of a redemption, or transformation, of time. Indeed, the apostle Paul, writing to the church in Ephesus, cautions them on precisely this point: "Therefore be careful how you walk, not as unwise,…but as wise, making the most of your time [or, literally, "redeeming the time"], because the days are evil" (Eph. 5:15–16).

So it is with the phrase "life everlasting" in the creed. The word *everlasting* is an adjective describing "life"; but as a descriptor, it means much more than the extension of time into infinity. Anyone who has sat through a long, boring sermon on an empty stomach knows that merely because an event lasts a long time does not mean that the event is a positive experience! The word *everlasting* carries as much of a qualitative meaning as it does a quantitative meaning. Everlasting refers not to a monotonous, unending existence, but a redeemed existence. When the creed refers to "life everlasting" it is pointing to an "'abundance' of life, overflowing, or excess of life"; it is life that stands against and is "unrestricted by death."[12] As Jesus says, "I came that they might have life, and might have it abundantly" (Jn. 10:10). For Andy, the Pacific Ocean does not have to remain "out there," nor does he have to leave Mozart on the record player; he can take Mozart with him. These are both symbols for a hope that breaks into time and transforms it, even when it is spent in a dark, dank, solitary cell.

2. Eternal life as a *"redemption of life."* After the suicide of Brooks Hatlen, Red comments on the destructive effects of prison life: "They send you here for life, and that's exactly what they take…the part that counts anyway." Once again, as a contrast, Andy symbolizes the power of hope to stand against that which robs life— both physically and spiritually. Not only does hope redeem Andy's life, hope inevitably restores life to Red. Red considers breaking parole and returning to prison or perhaps going the route of Brooks. But the hope contained in Andy's promise of something better is irresistible, and Red decides to follow Andy's advice, "Get busy living or get busy dying." Red chooses life.

Perhaps the most powerful image of rebirth and new life in *The Shawshank Redemption* is the scene where, having crawled through five hundred yards of sewage, Andy stands victorious, stripped bare in the pouring rain.[13] This, of course, is the second time in the film that we have seen Andy's bare body, and in both cases the symbolism is that of a stripping away of the old and preparation for the new. The first is when he is being hosed down just after entering prison. In both cases, Red narrates the scenes in connection with birth. In describing entrance into prison life, Red says, "They march you in naked as the day you were born," and in narrating the escape, he says that Andy "came out at the other end as fresh and clean as a newborn baby." In each scene, nakedness is a visual metaphor for birth, or rebirth—a transition from the old to the new. Similarly, the apostle Paul uses the metaphor of childbirth to describe the hope by which the Spirit is liberating not only humanity, but creation as a whole:

> For we know that the whole creation groans and suffers the pains of childbirth together until now. And not only this, but also we ourselves, having the first fruits of the Spirit, even we ourselves groan within ourselves, waiting eagerly for our adoption as [sons and daughters], the redemption of our body. For in hope we have been saved. (Rom. 8:22–23)

To hope for "life everlasting," then, is far more than sitting back in our church pews, dreaming of a heavenly mansion in the clouds. Loyalty to the life-giving, recreating, liberating Holy Spirit means actively standing against death and the powers of domination that deal in death. To live in loyalty to the Spirit is to "choose life" (Deut. 30:19), to actively work against poverty, war, murder, and violence in all their forms. Such a stance is not utopian or idealistic, for the Christian believes there is nothing more realistic than hope. As theologian Jürgen Moltmann says, "Hope alone is to be called 'realistic,' because it alone takes seriously the possibilities with which all reality is fraught...the despair which imagines it has reached the end of its tether proves to be illusory, as long as nothing has yet come to an end but everything is still full of possibilities."[14] For the Christian, hope is grounded in the victory of life over death already accomplished in the resurrection of Jesus of Nazareth. That is why Easter is always both a celebration and a protest—a celebration of life and a protest against death. Indeed, the Christian life is a life lived within that very contradiction. "That is why faith, wherever it develops into hope, causes not rest, but unrest, not patience, but impatience...Those who hope in Christ can no longer put up with reality as it is."[15]

There is much about the future that we do not know. The effort by some Christians to try to predict the future or to explain what will happen step-by-step, date-by-date, far from being an expression of Christian hope, is actually a form of hopelessness—an attempt to reduce mysterious possibility to cold science. What we *do* know as Christians is that whatever happens, our future is secure in the hands of God because of what has happened in Jesus of Nazareth. As John says, "It has not appeared as yet what we shall be." We do know, however, that "we shall be like Him" (1 Jn. 3:2).

QUESTIONS FOR DISCUSSION

1. What do you think is the "redemption" that takes place in *The Shawshank Redemption?*
2. How, if at all, do you see "hope" as a recurrent theme in the film and in the character of Andy Dufresne?
3. Do you see any religious symbolism at work in the film? If so, what role does it play?
4. The Apostles' Creed refers to "the resurrection of the body" and "the life everlasting." Do you see either of these symbolized at all in the film? What comes to your mind when you hear these phrases? What do you think they mean?

RELATED FILMS

Awakenings (1990)
Cries and Whispers (1972)
Ghost (1990)
The Lion King (1994)
Logan's Run (1976)
Ordet (1955)
Places in the Heart (1984)
The Rapture (1991)
Resurrection (1980)
Slaughterhouse Five (1972)
Star Trek III: The Search for Spock (1984)
Wings of Desire (1988)

NOTES

[1]Jürgen Moltmann expresses this splendidly when he says, "Does this hope cheat [us] of the happiness of the present? How could it do so! For it is itself the happiness of the present...Expectation makes life good, for in expectation, [we] can accept [our] whole present and find joy not only in its joy but also in its pain. Thus hope goes on its way through the midst of happiness and pain, because in the promises of God it can see a future also for the transient, the dying, and the dead. That is why it can be said that living without hope is like no longer living. Hell is hopelessness, and it is not for nothing that at the entrance to Dante's hell there stand the words: 'Abandon hope, all ye who enter here.'" *Theology of Hope* (New York: Harper & Row, 1967), 32.

[2]Stephen Schurr, "Shawshank's Redemption: How a Movie Found an Afterlife," *Wall Street Journal* (April 30, 1999), B4.

[3]Ibid., B1.

[4]Jewett, *Saint Paul Returns to the Movies*, 162.

[5]*Phaedo*, sections 116–18, as quoted in Will Durant, *The Story of Philosophy* (New York: Simon & Schuster, 1926), 12.

[6]Ibid., 11.

[7]See, for example, *Life* (1999), *No Escape* (1994), *Stir Crazy* (1980), *Escape From Alcatraz* (1979), or *The Great Escape* (1963).

[8]Contrast this with Robert Jewett's statement, "The metal box under the rock in Buxton is the most eloquent metaphor I have found in contemporary cinema for the 'hope' that we await in 'perseverance.'" *Saint Paul Returns to the Movies*, 169. This, however, still locates hope "out there" and opens hope to escapist and entirely futuristic interpretations.

[9]Robert Jewett compares this episode to the second of two baptisms that Andy receives. The first is his hosing down along with the other inmates, a washing away of the old life of freedom and initiation into a dehumanizing institution. The second, of course, is the reversal of the first. *Saint Paul Returns to the Movies*, 175.

[10]Roger Ebert, *Chicago Sun-Times*, September 23, 1994.

[11]Joan Ellis, *Nebbadoon, Inc.* Cf. Desson Howe, *Washington Post*, September 23, 1994.

[12]Jennings, *Loyalty to God*, 221.

[13]A baptismal image according to Jewett, *Saint Paul Returns to the Movies*, 174–75.

[14]Moltmann, *Theology of Hope*, 25.

[15]Ibid., 21.

Film Summaries

Babette's Feast (1987, NR, Drama, 102 minutes). In Danish and French with English subtitles. Director, Gabriel Axel. Starring: Stephane Audran. Academy Award winner for Best Foreign Language Film.

Contact (1997, PG-13, Science Fiction, 153 minutes). In English. Director, Robert Zemeckis. Starring: Jodie Foster, Matthew McConaughey, Tom Skerritt, James Woods. Academy Award nominated for Best Sound.

Dead Man Walking (1995, R, Drama, 122 minutes). In English. Director, Tim Robbins. Starring: Susan Sarandon, Sean Penn. Academy Award winner for Best Actress (Susan Sarandon). Academy Award nominated for Best Actor (Sean Penn), Director, and Song.

E. T. The Extra-Terrestrial (1982, PG, Science Fiction, 115 minutes). In English. Director, Steven Spielberg. Starring: Dee Wallace, Henry Thomas, Drew Barrymore. Academy Award winner for Best Original Score, Sound, Sound Effects, and Visual Effects. Academy Award nominated for Best Picture, Director, Screenplay, Cinematography, and Film Editing.

Flatliners (1990, R, Horror, 105 minutes). In English. Director, Joel Schumacher. Starring: Kiefer Sutherland, Julia Roberts, Kevin Bacon, William Baldwin, Oliver Platt. Academy Award nominated for Best Sound Effects.

The Gospel According to St. Matthew (1966, NR, Religious Drama, 133 minutes). In Italian with English subtitles (dubbed versions are also available). Director, Pier Paolo Pasolini. Starring: Enrique Irazoqui. Academy Award nominated for Best Art Direction/ Set Direction, Costume Design, and Music.

The Greatest Story Ever Told (1965, NR, Religious Drama, 141 minutes). In English. Director, George Stevens. Starring: Max von Sydow, Charlton Heston, José Ferrer, Donald Pleasance. Academy Award nominated for Best Art Direction/Set Direction, Cinematography, Costume Design, Musical Score, and Special Visual Effects.

Jesus of Montreal (1989, R, Drama, 119 minutes). In French with English subtitles. Director, Denys Arcand. Starring: Lothaire Bluteau, Catherine Wilkening. Academy Award nominated for Best Foreign Language Film.

The Last Temptation of Christ (1988, R, 164 minutes). In English. Director, Martin Scorsese. Starring: Willem Dafoe, Harvey Keitel, Barbara Hershey. Academy Award nominated for Best Director.

The Mission (1986, PG, Drama, 125 minutes). In English. Director, Roland Joffé. Starring: Robert De Niro, Jeremy Irons. Academy Award winner for Best Cinematography. Academy Award nominated for Best Picture, Director, Art Direction/Set Direction, Costume Design, Film Editing, and Original Music Score.

Oh, God! (1977, PG, Comedy, 104 minutes). In English. Director, Carl Reiner. Starring: George Burns, John Denver, Teri Garr. Acadamy Award nominated for Best Screenplay.

One Flew Over the Cuckoo's Nest (1975, R, Drama, 133 minutes). In English. Director, Miloš Forman. Starring: Jack Nicholson, Louise Fletcher, Will Sampson, Brad Dourif. Academy Award winner for Best Picture, Director, Adapted Screenplay, Actor (Jack Nicholson), and Actress (Louise Fletcher). Academy Award nominated for Best Supporting Actor, Cinematography, Film Editing, and Original Score.

Phenomenon (1996, PG, Drama, 124 minutes). In English. Director, John Turteltaub. Starring: John Travolta, Kyra Sedgwick, Forest Whitaker, Robert Duvall.

Powder (1995, PG–13, Fantasy/Drama, 111 minutes). In English. Director, Victor Salva. Starring: Sean Patrick Flanery, Mary Steenburgen, Lance Henriksen, Jeff Goldblum.

Romero (1989, PG–13, Biography/Drama, 102 minutes). In English. Director, John Duigan. Starring: Raul Julia, Richard Jordan, Ana Alicia, Tony Plana.

The Shawshank Redemption (1994, R, Drama, 142 minutes). In English. Director, Frank Darabont. Starring: Tim Robbins, Morgan Freeman, Bob Gunton, William Sadler, James Whitmore. Academy Award nominated for Best Picture, Actor (Morgan

Freeman), Screenplay, Cinematography, Film Editing, Original Score, and Sound.

Star Wars (1977, PG, Science Fiction, 121 minutes). In English. Director, George Lucas. Starring: Mark Hamill, Harrison Ford, Carrie Fisher. Academy Award winner for Art Direction, Costume Design, Film Editing, Original Score, Visual Effects, and Special Achievement for Sound Effects. Academy Award Nominated for Best Picture, Director, Supporting Actor, and Screenplay.

2001: A Space Odyssey (1968, PG, Science Fiction, 139 minutes). In English. Director, Stanley Kubrick. Starring: Keir Dullea, Gary Lockwood, William Sylvester. Academy Award winner for Best Special Visual Effects. Academy Award nominated for Best Director, Screenplay, and Art Direction.

Index

Printed in the United States
64188LVS00002B/1-99